Breaking the Romans Code

Breaking the Romans Code

Michael Wood

Tubi Publishing, LLC

Breaking the Romans Code

ISBN: 978-1-936565-09-2 (pbk)

ISBN: 978-1-936565-10-8 (hrc)

ISBN: 978-1-936565-11-5 (ebk)

Printed in the United States of America

Contents

Acknowledgments

To Esteban Serrano and Osvaldo Jerez whose constant support and encouragement has made this work possible.

To Ralph Schulz whose critique and feedback challenged me to bring this manuscript to a much higher level.

To Jaime Alberto Castano and Juan David Yanes whose willingness to critique so many revisions helped fine tune many important distinctions.

Introducing Biblical Cryptanalysis

Chapter 1
Breakthrough

Early in my career life I was honored to receive international recognition for designing REDOC-II which is one of the only unbreakable codes in existence today.[1, 2, 3] At the time I had no idea that my early accomplishments in cryptography would ever provide me with a unique approach to Biblical archaeology. Yet the skillset of making and breaking codes enabled me to ultimately solve a two-thousand-year-old puzzle.

Here's how it all began. After designing the unbreakable code I was given an opportunity to apply my cryptanalytic skills to the emerging internet field. I transformed a cryptanalysis system that I had developed into programmable artificial intelligence. The resulting software instructed a computer how to decipher the information flowing through its network wires. The computer then transformed the deciphered information into a real-time blueprint of the entire worldwide physical infrastructure.[4] Maintaining a real-time map of the network was critical to effectively manage the rapidly changing

1 The Redoc-II Encryption System (US Patent #5,003,596)

2 See *Applied Cryptography* by Bruce Schneier, pp. 311-313 for an overview of the REDOC-II code and documentation of its impenetrability.

3 The two Israelis who broke the United States' standard national code (the DES) confirmed they were unable to break REDOC-II via their method. REDOC-II proved not only to be superior to the code developed by the US National Security Agency—it proved to be unbreakable. See Eli Biham and Adi Shamir, Differential Cryptanalysis of Snefru, Khafre, REDOC-II, LOKI and Lucifer. Advances in Cryptology -- CRYPTO '91, Springer-Verlag, pp. 156–171

4 US Patent #6,108,702

infrastructure. The commercial success of this system provided the opportunity for early retirement, during which I turned my cryptanalytic attention to some personal areas of interest.

For example, I had always been intrigued by the human nervous system. The parasympathetic nerves (which shut off the stress response) cause subtle changes in the human heart rate. Through cryptanalysis I was able to use heart rate measurements to decode the precise real time level of parasympathetic activity. The cryptanalytic solution was imbedded within a stress reducing biofeedback device.[5] The device has shown impressive results in multiple clinical trials.[6, 7, 8, 9, 10, 11]

The three cryptanalytic breakthroughs provided me the experience necessary to finally tackle one of the greatest historical puzzles of them all—decoding the mysteries of the Dead Sea Scrolls. I had a particular fascination with the scrolls found in cave four, because their publication was suppressed for so long. They were eventually published in 1991 by force, not willingly. And I was always curious what earth-shattering things they must contain for them to have been kept under wrap for so many decades.

However, the hoopla surrounding these scrolls quickly died down after their release for two reasons. First, no one noticed anything remarkable in them. And second, the official story caught on: "There

5 US Patent #7,691,049

6 "Effects of Respiratory Sinus Arrhythmia Biofeedback Versus Passive Biofeedback Control," Leslie Sherlin, Richard Gevirtz, Sarah Wyckoff, Fred Muench, International Journal of Stress Management, 2009, Vol. 16, No. 3, 233–248

7 "The Effects of Respiratory Sinus Arrhythmia Biofeedback on Heart Rate Variability and Posttraumatic Stress Disorder Symptoms: A Pilot Study," Terri L. Zucker, Kristin W. Samuelson, Frederick Muench, Melanie A. Greenberg, Richard N. Gevirtz, Appl Psychophysiol Biofeedback, DOI 10.1007/s10484-009-9085-2

8 Prinsloo, GE, Rauch, HGL, Lambert, MI, Muench, F, Noakes, TD & Derman WE (2010). The Effect of Short Duration Heart Rate Variability (HRV) Biofeedback on Cognitive Performance During Laboratory Induced Cognitive Stress. Appl. Cognit. Psychol. wileyonlinelibrary.com DOI: 10.1002 acp 1750

9 Ebben, MR, Kurbatov, V & Pollak, CP (2009). Moderating Laboratory Adaptation with the Use of a Heart-Rate Variability Biofeedback Device (StressEraser). Appl Psychophysiol Biofeedback, DOI 10.1007/s10484-009-9086-1

10 Reiner, R (2008). Integrating a Portable Biofeedback Device into Clinical Practice for Patients with Anxiety Disorders: Results of a Pilot Study, Appl Psychophysiol Biofeedback, 33, 55-61.

11 Heilman, K, Handelman, M, Lewis, G & Porges, SW (2008). Accuracy of the StressEraser® in the Detection of Cardiac Rhythms, Appl Psychophysiol Biofeedback, 33(2), 83-89.

never was a cover up in the first place. It just took that long to translate them because of the extra fragility of the cave four scrolls."

But the official response only served to pique my curiosity even further. The cave four scholars had completed a handwritten concordance of the scrolls by 1960,[12] and the scholars had to translate the scrolls in order to make the concordance. The concordance was empirical proof that the official story was itself a cover up. The scrolls were translated by 1960, yet remained unpublished for more than thirty years afterwards.

I pored through the cave four scrolls for about a decade. During that time, my background allowed me to piece together some historic findings. But only recently did I discover the Granddaddy of the cave four secrets. And that is what led to the writing of this book.

Paul's letter to the Romans is the cornerstone of modern Christianity. A correct understanding of the book relies on knowing exactly what Paul was referring to by the phrase 'Works of the Law.' And archeologists discovered a scroll in cave four entitled "Some Works of the Law." This was the first time the idiomatic phrase was seen outside of Paul's letters. Something inside me was convinced this held the key to the ultimate surprise regarding the Biblical book of Romans.

When taken in combination with Paul's letter to the Romans, the scroll shows that the phrase 'Works of the Law' was a first century idiom used to refer to a specific subset of the Law. Yet the scroll was written by a religious sect called the Essenes, and Paul was trained as a Pharisee (under the tutelage of Gamaliel).[13] So I sought to understand how the Pharisees used the idiom. Which subset of the Law did that phrase represent to them?

The breakthrough arrived the moment I came across the traditional Pharisaic legal divisions: *mitzvot bein adam lamakom* (commands between man and God) and *mitzvot bein adam lachaveiro* (commands between man and his neighbor). These were the original

12 *The Complete Dead Sea Scrolls in English* by Geza Vermes, p. 5

13 Acts 22:3. NOTE: Gamaliel was the grandson of Hillel, the founder of the highly regarded Pharisaic School of Hillel.

two subsets at the time of Christ and my cryptanalytic mind began snapping together all the pieces of the puzzle. Not only did the completed puzzle reveal a stunning revelation about the book of Romans, but it also forever changes Christianity's understanding of Jesus' teachings as well. The original teaching of Romans is finally revealed. The code has been broken.

Chapter 2
Insufficient Inputs

In this book, we're going to use a revolutionary new method to understand the Bible: Biblical Cryptanalysis. Now, if you are skeptical that any new approach can yield historic results, I acknowledge and respect your reservations. After all, how can a new method uncover anything remarkable about the most analyzed text on the planet? Actually, there's a straightforward cryptographic answer to that question.

All codes, even the easiest ones, require a sufficient number of inputs before they can be solved. If a cryptographer is handed the most simplistic child's code and only a small number of input/output pairs, he still won't be able to determine the key until he has more inputs. Biblical scholars have been in a similar situation with Jesus' teachings for fifteen hundred years. Even though tremendously gifted scholars existed during these times, they've been operating off a limited number of inputs—too few to find the key. Mostly, they were missing information regarding first century Jewish culture and Law.

For example, consider the ancient Jewish idiom "to have an evil eye." Today's English meaning for "evil eye" is extremely different from the ancient Jewish one. In first century Judea to "have an evil eye" meant "to be stingy" and "to have a good eye" meant "to be generous." The idiom was based on eyeing material things over the needs of others. Those with a bad eye focus on the material things.[14, 15, 16] Those with a good eye focus on the needs of others.

With this in mind, let's take a look at how the seventeenth century King James Bible translated a sentence from Jesus' Sermon on the Mount.

> If thine eye be evil, thy whole body shall be full of darkness.[17]

The King James translation was the official Bible for almost three hundred years. So for three hundred years, Christians believed that Jesus warned against having an 'evil eye.' For three centuries, they didn't know that he was actually warning against being stingy—a different message altogether.

Before the King James Bible, the Latin Vulgate was the official Bible for almost thirteen hundred years. So how well did it do with this Hebraism?

> But if thy eye be evil thy whole body shall be darksome.[18]

Not well. The Latin Vulgate didn't grasp the idiom either. So between the Latin Vulgate and the King James Bible, Christians were told for fifteen hundred years that Jesus warned them not to fill their bodies with darkness by having an evil eye. For fifteen hundred years, Christians didn't know what Jesus actually taught:

> If your eye stingily focuses on material things, your whole body will be full of darkness.

John Calvin's writings show us how unaware the Protestant Reformers were regarding Jewish idioms. When Calvin commented on the "evil eye", he wrote:

---

14 *A Commentary on the Gospel of Matthew* by Craig S. Keener (Jul 1999) p. 232. (Craig S. Keener (PhD, Duke University) is professor of Biblical studies at Palmer Theological Seminary of Eastern University.)

15 *Eerdmans Dictionary of the Bible* by David Noel Freedman, Allen C. Myers, Astrid B. Beck, p. 498

16 *Dictionary of Jesus and the Gospels* (The IVP Bible Dictionary Series) by Joel B. Green, Scot McKnight, and I. Howard Marshall p. 472. (Joel B. Green is Dean of Academic Affairs at Asbury Theological Seminary and Professor of New Testament Interpretation.)

17 Matthew 6:23 KJV

18 Matthew 6:23 Latin Vulgate

> An evil eye means a diseased eye … they shut their eyes to avoid the light which was offered to them, because they are knowingly and willingly carried after their own lusts.[19]

Calvin wrote authoritatively. Calvin wrote charismatically. Calvin wrote with conviction. And yet, Calvin was wrong. Again, it's not his fault. He wrote in an information vacuum and did the best he could. But unfortunately, one error begets another … creating a negative feedback loop. By not knowing that Jesus meant 'don't be stingy,' Calvin carried forward his own erroneous concept into his interpretation of what the "darkness" meant:

> darkness signifies gross and brutal affections. The meaning is, we ought not to wonder, if men wallow so disgracefully, like beasts, in the filth of vices, for they have no reason which might restrain the blind and dark lusts of the flesh.[20]

Jesus' "don't be stingy with your belongings" has now been turned into a warning against living "disgracefully, like beasts, in the filth of vices." The snowball is rolling downhill … fast.

The 'evil eye' passage was never a diatribe against filthy vices. Rather it was one of the most humanitarian passages in the entire Bible.

> Accumulate for yourselves treasures in heaven, where neither moth nor rust destroys, and where thieves do not break in or steal; for where your treasure is, there your heart will be also. The eye is the lamp of the body; so then if your eye generously focuses on the needs of others, your whole body will be full of light. But if your eye stingily focuses on material things, your whole body will be full of darkness.[21]

The passage discusses storing up treasures in heaven by generously sharing with those in need. In fact, this passage was seamlessly related to something that Jesus had taught before it:

> But when you give to the poor, do not let your left hand know what your right hand is doing, so that your giving will be in secret; and your Father who sees what is done in secret will reward you.[22]

---

19 *Commentary on Matthew, Mark, Luke* by John Calvin, entry for Matthew 6:22-24

20 *Commentary on Matthew, Mark, Luke* by John Calvin, entry for Matthew 6:22-24

21 Matthew 6:19-23

22 Matthew 6:3-4 NASB

Jesus had already discussed receiving a heavenly reward for generously sharing with those in need. And his first century audience understood how the "good eye vs. evil eye" seamlessly related to it.

But what happens when a person doesn't know the meaning of the "good eye vs. evil eye"? How can he possibly see the seamless fluidity of the passage? He cannot, as John Calvin illustrates. When commenting on "the eye is the lamp of the body", Calvin wrote:

> We must bear in mind, as I have already hinted, that what we find here are detached sentences, and not a continued discourse.[23]

This sentence is quite revealing. John Calvin had "already been hinting" that the entire sermon is a mishmash of "detached sentences, and not a continued discourse." His lack of knowledge regarding Hebraisms caused him to view the entire sermon as a set of detached, standalone, disconnected teachings.

Now let's think about this for a moment. As long as scholars didn't know what the "evil eye" referred to (say, for about fifteen hundred years), it was impossible for them to look for a single unified message in the Sermon on the Mount. After all, they already 'knew' the sermon was a bunch of "detached sentences, and not a continued discourse."

But it turns out that the "evil eye" wasn't disconnected at all. In fact, it was a virtual restatement of something that Jesus had just previously taught: People store up treasures in heaven when they generously share with those in need. So is it possible that the entire sermon is a continuous discourse after all? And if it is, how can we possibly recover its original seamless fluidity? That's where Biblical cryptanalysis comes in.

23 *Commentary on Matthew, Mark, Luke* by John Calvin, entry for Matthew 6:22-24

Chapter 3
Biblical Code Breaking

So what does cryptanalysis (the breaking of codes) have to do with the Bible anyway? Actually, it has everything to do with the Bible. Let's take a look at how a single new input combined with cryptanalysis can produce a historic result.

Jesus' Sermon on the Mount uses the Koine Greek word *dikaiosune* three times. And the Jewish audience that he was addressing had a special Hebraic understanding of this word. The Jewish communities used this word as a synonym for the Hebrew word *chesed* which meant 'loving kindness.' This can be traced back as far as 200 B.C. when the Jewish scriptures were translated into Greek. The ancient translators used the Greek word *dikaiosune* in some passages when translating the Hebrew word *chesed*.[24]

The Jewish use of *dikaiosune* as an expression of loving kindness continued to strengthen over time. By Jesus' day, *dikaiosune* was associated with charitable deeds done for others, such as giving alms to the poor.[25] In fact, Jesus himself used the word this way in his Sermon on the Mount:

> Beware of practicing your ***dikaiosune*** before men to be noticed by them; otherwise you have no reward with your Father who is in heaven. So **when you give to the poor**, do not sound a trumpet before you, as the hypocrites do in the synagogues and in the streets, so that they may be honored by

24 See Genesis 19:19, 20:13, 21:23, 24:27, 32:10 LXX

25 *Meet the Rabbis: Rabbinic Thought and the Teachings of Jesus* by Brad H. Young, pp. 9-10

> men truly I say to you, they have their reward in full. But **when you give to the poor**, do not let your left hand know what your right hand is doing,[26]

Giving alms to the poor was considered one of the highest acts of loving kindness. Notice that the passage describes this expression of loving kindness as "practicing your *dikaiosune*." Now that we understand how deeply the first century Jews equated *dikaiosune* with the kind treatment of others, we are ready to perform our first Biblical cryptanalysis.

The lengthy passage below is one of the more popular passages in the New Testament. I am going to demonstrate how one new input (*dikaiosune*) combined with cryptanalysis can result in a historic Biblical finding—the recovery of an essential teaching of Jesus', which had remained unknown for fifteen hundred years.

> For I say to you that unless your ***dikaiosune*** surpasses that of the scribes and Pharisees, you will not enter the kingdom of heaven.
>
> You have heard that the ancients were told, 'YOU SHALL NOT COMMIT MURDER' and 'Whoever commits murder shall be liable to the court.' But I say to you that everyone who is angry with his brother shall be guilty before the court; and whoever says to his brother, 'You good-for-nothing,' shall be guilty before the supreme court; and whoever says, 'You fool,' shall be guilty enough to go into the fiery hell.
>
> Therefore if you are presenting your offering at the altar, and there remember that your brother has something against you, leave your offering there before the altar and go; first be reconciled to your brother, and then come and present your offering. Make friends quickly with your opponent at law while you are with him on the way, so that your opponent may not hand you over to the judge, and the judge to the officer, and you be thrown into prison. Truly I say to you, you will not come out of there until you have paid up the last cent.
>
> You have heard that it was said, 'YOU SHALL NOT COMMIT ADULTERY'; but I say to you that everyone who looks at a woman with lust for her has already committed adultery with her in his heart. If your right eye makes you stumble, tear it out and throw it from you; for it is better for you to lose one of the parts of your body, than for your whole body to be thrown into hell. If your right hand makes you stumble, cut it off and throw it from you; for it is better for you to lose one of the parts of your body, than for your whole body to go into hell.

26 Matthew 6:1-3 NASB with *dikaiosune* left untranslated

> It was said, 'WHOEVER SENDS HIS WIFE AWAY, LET HIM GIVE HER A CERTIFICATE OF DIVORCE'; but I say to you that everyone who divorces his wife, except for the reason of unchastity, makes her commit adultery; and whoever marries a divorced woman commits adultery.
>
> Again, you have heard that the ancients were told, 'YOU SHALL NOT MAKE FALSE VOWS, BUT SHALL FULFILL YOUR VOWS TO THE LORD.' But I say to you, make no oath at all, either by heaven, for it is the throne of God, or by the earth, for it is the footstool of His feet, or by Jerusalem, for it is THE CITY OF THE GREAT KING. Nor shall you make an oath by your head, for you cannot make one hair white or black. But let your statement be, 'Yes, yes' or 'No, no'; anything beyond these is of evil.
>
> You have heard that it was said, 'AN EYE FOR AN EYE, AND A TOOTH FOR A TOOTH.' But I say to you, do not resist an evil person; but whoever slaps you on your right cheek, turn the other to him also. If anyone wants to sue you and take your shirt, let him have your coat also. Whoever forces you to go one mile, go with him two. Give to him who asks of you, and do not turn away from him who wants to borrow from you.
>
> You have heard that it was said, 'YOU SHALL LOVE YOUR NEIGHBOR and hate your enemy.' But I say to you, love your enemies and pray for those who persecute you, so that you may be sons of your Father who is in heaven; for He causes His sun to rise on the evil and the good, and sends rain on the righteous and the unrighteous. For if you love those who love you, what reward do you have? Do not even the tax collectors do the same? If you greet only your brothers, what more are you doing than others? Do not even the Gentiles do the same? Therefore you are to be perfect, as your heavenly Father is perfect.[27]

Before I reveal my cryptanalysis of this passage, let's take a look at what the first sentence means. The first sentence says:

> Unless your *dikaiosune* is greater than the religious leaders you cannot enter the kingdom of heaven.

And from our knowledge of the *dikaiosune* Hebraism, we know this sentence means:

> Unless you treat people better than the religious leaders you cannot enter the kingdom of heaven.

By combining just one new input (*dikiosune*) with Biblical cryptanalysis, we recover the lost meaning of the passage:

27 Matthew 5:20-48 NASB with *dikaiosune* left untranslated.

- You have heard 'don't murder' and 'those who murder shall be liable to the court.'
    - **But I tell you that you have to treat people better than that.** Anyone who is angry with his brother is liable to the court and anyone who calls his brother a name is in danger of hellfire.
- You have heard 'don't commit adultery.'
    - **But I tell you that you have to treat people better than that.** Don't ogle a woman lustfully with your eyes or you're already an adulterer. It would be better for you to have no eyes if you can't stop offending your wife and the woman you are ogling.
- It was said that anyone can divorce his wife simply by giving her a certificate of divorce.
    - **But I tell you that you have to treat people better than that.** You can only divorce a woman if she's been unfaithful to you. And anyone who marries the divorced unfaithful woman shares in her adultery.
- You have heard the ancients were told not to make false vows, but to fulfill vows to the Lord.
    - **But I tell you that you have to treat people better than that.** Just keep your word even without oaths. Let your 'yes' be 'yes' and your 'no' be 'no.' Period.
- You have heard 'an eye for an eye, and a tooth for a tooth.'
    - **But I tell you that you have to treat people better than that.** Don't take revenge on a person who injures you. Offer him assistance instead.

- You have heard that you should love your countrymen and hate your enemies.
    - **But I tell you that you have to treat people better than that.** You need to love your enemies and pray for those who harm you. Otherwise you will not reap the reward.

Now think about what Biblical cryptanalysis has already done. We've unified twenty-nine sentences via a single statement, and we've uncovered the lost meaning of the passage as a result. The passage had always been describing how a first century Jew could treat his neighbor better than what his religion taught; nothing more, nothing less. This opens up an entirely new understanding about Jesus and his message.

Let's take divorce as an example. In the first century, many religious leaders allowed a man to divorce his wife if he found her displeasing in any way.[28] Women were sent away at the whim of their husbands. Jesus wanted the husbands to treat their wives better than that. *That's* why Jesus implemented his rule. He also didn't want women to use his unfaithfulness clause to break their marriage to be with another man. He wanted the wife to treat her husband better than that. So he said that all women who are divorced under his standard of adultery can't remarry.

The motivation behind all the rules was to get his followers to start treating *everyone* better ... even women ... even foreign enemies. It's actually a beautiful passage once the code has been cracked.

28 *Meet the Rabbis: Rabbinic Thought and the Teachings of Jesus* by Brad H. Young, p. 41

Chapter 4
The Key

In cryptography, we know that we've found the key to a code when the following happens:

All known inputs + Key = Intelligible output

When all the inputs combined with the key result in intelligible output, we know we are done… we know that we have found the key. In the last chapter, we found a single statement which accounted for all twenty-nine sentences (all twenty-nine inputs). And when we combined all twenty-nine inputs with that singular statement, we got a magnified level of intelligible output. So we're done (with that passage). We've found the key.

But think what this means. For fifteen hundred years, no one knew what Jesus had actually taught: Unless you treat people better than the religious leaders, you cannot enter the kingdom of heaven. No one knew this particular passage taught that love of neighbor is the prerequisite to entering the kingdom of heaven. No one knew that all twenty-nine sentences contributed together to convey this one singular message.

So research into first century Jewish culture combined with old fashioned cryptanalysis yielded a historic result—and this is just one teaching. Imagine what we might discover if we found the key to the entire Sermon on the Mount! If we could find a single statement that accounts for the sermon from beginning to end, then perhaps we'll discover that the entire sermon is very different from what Christians thought for fifteen hundred years.

What if we sought to find the key to all of Jesus' teachings on salvation and judgment in the Gospel of Matthew? Would we find that Jesus' salvation teachings were different than what Christians have thought for fifteen hundred years?

What about Paul's letter to the Romans: Is it even possible to find a single statement that encompasses every sentence in this lengthy letter from beginning to end? And if we did, would we find that the Biblical book that modern Christianity is based upon actually teaches something different than what Christians thought for fifteen hundred years?

Armed with new knowledge regarding first century culture and law, we have sufficient inputs to finally solve these three massive puzzles:

Puzzle #1: The Sermon on the Mount

Puzzle #2: The Gospel of Matthew

Puzzle #3: Romans

As you will soon see, a whole host of Biblical surprises reveal themselves at every twist and turn in solving these puzzles. Christianity is about to discover that the most essential teaching (The Sermon on the Mount) and the most essential Biblical books (Matthew and Romans) are extremely different from what Christians believed for fifteen hundred years. And Biblical cryptanalysis is going to prove it.

Puzzle #1

The Sermon on the Mount

Chapter 5
The Set Up

Jesus' Sermon on the Mount is recorded in the Gospel of Matthew. This Gospel was written by a first century Jew for a first century Jewish audience. It is drenched in Jewish idioms and ideology. Jesus' opening statement to his Sermon on the Mount is a great example of this.

> **Do not think that I came to abolish the Law or the Prophets; I did not come to abolish but to fulfill.** For truly I say to you, **until heaven and earth pass away, not the smallest letter or stroke shall pass from the Law** until all is accomplished. Whoever then annuls one of **the least of these commandments**, and teaches others to do the same, **shall be called least** in **the kingdom of heaven**; but **whoever keeps** and teaches them, he **shall be called great** in **the kingdom of heaven.**[29]

In each of the bolded words above, Jesus made use of a common Jewish idiom or ideology. That's how entrenched Hebraisms are in the Gospel of Matthew. Let's take a look at some of them.

the Law and the Prophets

The Law and the Prophets were the entire canonical scriptures for the Jews of Jesus' day.[30] So the first thing we notice is that Jesus is talking about *the entirety of Jewish scripture.*

---

29 Matthew 5:17-19 NASB

30 "The canonization of the *Ketuvim* began in 65 C.E. and was not completed until about 140 C.E." *A Rabbinic Commentary on the New Testament* by Samuel Tobias Lachs, p. 87. Thus, only the Law and the Prophets were biblical canon at the time Jesus delivered his Sermon on the Mount.

Let's look at another one:

> I did not come to abolish but to fulfill.

Jesus used an extremely common religious idiom when he contrasted 'abolishing the Law and the Prophets' vs. 'fulfilling the Law and the Prophets.' When a religious teacher felt a colleague had nullified a commandment by his interpretation of scripture, he would accuse him of 'abolishing the scripture.' It was up to the accused to show that he was 'fulfilling the scripture'—preserving every single commandment in his interpretation.[31]

Brad H. Young[32] put it this way:

> Jesus does not say that he intends to render the Law obsolete. Rather he seeks to strengthen it through proper interpretation and application.[33]

So Jesus introduced his sermon by promising to give an interpretation of scripture, which doesn't annul a single commandment. And then he emphasized this point even further:

> not the smallest letter or stroke shall pass from the Law

The Hebrew and Koine Greek languages don't just use letters, but they also employ tiny symbols formed by the stroke of a pen. These are called accent and breathing marks, and Jesus was referring to them here. He was saying that his interpretation is going to be so complete, that it includes preserving not just the letters, but the accents and breathing marks around them as well. Clearly, he's building up to something, because he's setting the stage in quite a dramatic fashion.

One would think that Jesus had driven home his point far enough. Yet he pressed it further still:

> until heaven and earth pass away

---

31 *The New Testament and Rabbinic Judaism* by David Daube, pp. 60-61. Note: Who's Who lists David Daube as the twentieth century's preeminent scholar of ancient Law (including Roman law and ancient Jewish Law).

32 Brad H. Young earned his M.A. and Ph.D. degrees in Judaism and Early Christianity at Hebrew University, Jerusalem, Israel where he studied for ten years. Mr. Young currently serves as a professor of New Testament Studies in the Graduate School of Theology at Oral Roberts University.

33 *Meet the Rabbis: Rabbinic Thought and the Teachings of Jesus* by Brad H. Young, p. 43.

Here Jesus appeals to another very common first century Jewish understanding, as Jesus' contemporary, Philo Judaeus, shows:

> The Law is immortal as long as the sun and moon and the whole heaven and universe exist.[34]

Jesus promised to give an interpretation of scripture that will not annul a single commandment. In fact, he promised his interpretation will preserve all the letters (and even the accents and breathing marks) until the end of time. Then he declared that because his interpretation preserves the Law until the end of time, all his followers are required to keep the whole thing down to the smallest detail:

> Whoever then annuls one of the least of these commandments, and teaches others to do the same, shall be called least in the kingdom of heaven; but whoever keeps and teaches them, he shall be called great in the kingdom of heaven.

Once again, Jesus was appealing to a common Jewish ideal. Consider how similar his words are to Rabbi Judah the Prince, a prominent second century Pharisee:

> Be just as heedful of a light commandment as a heavy one, for you do not know the amount of reward for each commandment.[35]

How strange it must be for the modern Christian to know that Jesus ties the amount of reward to keeping all the commandments down to the smallest one. Yet that is precisely what he said. In a nutshell, Jesus introduced his Sermon on the Mount by saying:

> I haven't come to annul a single commandment in scripture. Rather I have come to give an interpretation of scripture that preserves every command (down to the smallest letter and even the decorative marks) until the end of time. Therefore, the amount of your reward in the kingdom depends on how well you follow all the commandments, even the seemingly insignificant ones.

The Jewish audience must have been wondering why Jesus repeated the same thing over and over again. Why did he keep repeating that his interpretation encompasses every single commandment down

34 *The Life of Moses* by Philo, 2.3.

35 Mishna Avot 2.1 (an ancient Jewish writing)

to the tiniest one? Little did they know, Jesus just set them up...

Chapter 6
Yanking the Carpet

The early Jewish sages divided the commandments of the Law into two distinct subsets: *mitzvot bein adam lamakom* (commands between man and God) and *mitzvot bein adam lachaveiro* (commands between man and his neighbor).

As Robert Gordis[36] explains:

> The Jewish law[37], however, like the Torah itself, is not limited to ethical conduct, *mitzvot bein adam lachaveiro*, "commandments between man and man." In fact, much of Jewish law deals with ritual and ceremony, *mitzvot bein adam lamakom*, "commandments between man and God."[38]

Yes, there were two divisions. Yes, much of the Law dealt with ritual and ceremony. And yes, the commandments between man and God were considered the most important. Yet, after promising to give an interpretation of the Law and the Prophets that didn't annul a single commandment, Jesus drops a bombshell at the end of the sermon:

> In everything, therefore, treat others the same way you want to be treated for this is the Law and the Prophets. Come enter through the narrow gate.

36 Robert Gordis served as President of the Rabbinical Assembly and the Synagogue Council of America and was a professor at Jewish Theological Seminary of America from 1940 to 1992. He was a highly influential conservative rabbi and scholar.

37 Robert Gordis uses the Hebraic word *Halakhah* here which means "the Jewish Law."

38 *The Dynamics of Judaism: A Study in Jewish Law* by Robert Gordis, p. 63

Can you imagine the ruckus? After all, were there two divisions in Jesus' interpretation? No. Did his interpretation include any ritual and ceremony? No. Were the commandments between man and God the most important? No, they weren't even included.

But didn't Jesus promise not to annul a single commandment down to the tiniest one? Yes, he did. And that's the point! In first century Jewish speak, Jesus dropped a bomb: *I haven't come to abolish the Law and the Prophets because only the neighbor-based commands are the Law and the Prophets.*

Now we know why the Sermon on the Mount was a profound history-changing shocker. Jesus of Nazareth discarded one subset of the Law while leaving the other subset fully intact. Jesus discarded the commands between man and God (*mitzvot bein adam lamakom*) while leaving the commands between man and neighbor (*mitzvot bein adam lachaveiro*) fully intact. In no uncertain terms, he declared that the commands between man and God were never Law in the first place. *This* is what sent shockwaves throughout first century Judea.

"But wait!" you may protest. "There are a whole lot of teachings between the initial setup and his conclusion."

Yes, there most certainly are. So let's see if there's a key (a single statement) that accounts for every sentence between the initial setup and the titillating conclusion. And let's see if that key weakens the conclusion … or reinforces it seven times over.

Chapter 7
The Body Eclectic

The body of the Sermon on the Mount is comprised of the following seven teachings:

The Body of Jesus'
Sermon on the Mount

1. Only if you treat people better than the scribes and the Pharisees can you enter the kingdom of heaven. (Matthew 5:20-48)
2. Your Father in heaven will reward you when you secretly give to the poor. (Matthew 6:1-4)
3. God will forgive your sins in direct proportion to your forgiveness of others. (Matthew 6:5-15)
4. You store up treasures in heaven by generously sharing with those in need. (Matthew 6:19-24)
5. Don't worry about your own needs. Just focus on bringing God's kingdom to earth by expressing loving kindness[39] and God will meet your needs as well. (Matthew 6:25-34)
6. Whatever measure you use on others, God will use on you. (Matthew 7:1-6)

39 This teaching uses the Hebraic idiom *dikaiosune,* which referred to expressing loving kindness. See Chapter 3, "Biblical Code Breaking," for details.

7. Treat others well, because as a child of God,[40] your heavenly Father will give you far greater rewards than you can possibly give even to your own family. (Matthew 7:7-11)

Now that we've organized the sermon into a manageable structure, we're ready to find the key. We're ready to find a single statement that accounts for all seven teachings (and thereby, every sentence between the introduction and the surprising conclusion).

The cryptanalytic answer is given below:

The Key to the Body of Jesus' Sermon on the Mount

1. **God is going to treat you based on how you treat others.** Therefore, only if you treat people better than the scribes and the Pharisees can you enter the kingdom of heaven. (Matthew 5:20-48)
2. **God is going to treat you based on how you treat others.** Therefore, your Father in heaven will reward you when you secretly give to the poor. (Matthew 6:1-4)
3. **God is going to treat you based on how you treat others.** Therefore, God will forgive your sins in direct proportion to your forgiveness of others. (Matthew 6:5-15)
4. **God is going to treat you based on how you treat others.** Therefore, you store up treasures in heaven by generously sharing with those in need. (Matthew 6:19-24)
5. **God is going to treat you based on how you treat others.** Therefore, don't worry about your own needs. Just focus on bringing God's kingdom to earth by expressing loving kindness[41] and God will meet your needs as well. (Matthew 6:25-34)
6. **God is going to treat you based on how you treat others.** Therefore, whatever measure you use on others, God will use on you. (Matthew 7:1-6)

---

40 Jesus already stated in Matthew 5:44-45 that only those who love others are children of the heavenly Father. This is the prerequisite for being in the adoptive position of receiving gifts from the heavenly Father.

41 This teaching uses the Hebraic idiom *dikaiosune* which referred to expressing loving kindness. See Chapter 3, "Biblical Code Breaking," for details.

7. **God is going to treat you based on how you treat others.** Therefore, treat others well, because as a child of God,[42] your heavenly Father will give you far greater rewards than you can possibly give even to your own family. (Matthew 7:7-11)

Jesus used the body of the sermon to repeat a single principle seven times over: *God is going to treat you based on how you treat others.* The teachings of the body provide the theological basis for the conclusion:

- *Introduction* - I promise to give an interpretation of the Law and the Prophets that preserves every commandment down to the smallest one.

- *Body* - God is going to treat you based on the way you treat others.

- *Conclusion* - Therefore, treating others the same way that you want to be treated is the entire Law and the Prophets.

Now we can see why insufficient inputs made finding the key impossible for so many centuries. How could scholars find the key when they had to put 'don't have an evil eye which neglects guidance of affections' into the mix? How could scholars find the key when they had to include 'don't wallow so disgracefully, like beasts, in the filth of vices?' It was impossible for scholars to find the key for many centuries. They had insufficient inputs.

The insufficient inputs created a negative feedback loop, causing them to conclude that Jesus' sermon was a discontinuous set of free-floating ideas and instructions.[43] Therefore, they didn't even look for a key which could encompass it all, for they had already concluded that such a thing couldn't possibly exist.

But now, everything's changed. We finally have enough inputs to solve the entire puzzle. How do we know that we have enough inputs? Let me ask you a question: When you bring home a puzzle, how do you know when you've solved it? Simple, once the assembly

42 Jesus already stated in Matthew 5:44-45 that only those who love others are children of the heavenly Father. This is the prerequisite for being in the adoptive position of receiving gifts from the heavenly Father.

43 John Calvin wrote that he considered the sermon as a whole to be a conglomeration of "detached sentences, and not a continued discourse." See Commentary on *Matthew, Mark, Luke* by John Calvin, entry for Matthew 6:22-24.

contains all the pieces, you know that you've solved the puzzle. You know you are done. Likewise, the moment our assembly of the Sermon on the Mount contains all the pieces, we know that we are done.

So, are we finished? Not quite. The entire sermon is composed of five sections:

1. Beatitudes
2. Introduction
3. Body
4. Conclusion
5. Warnings

We've discussed everything so far but the warnings. So how do the warnings contribute to the sermon?

Chapter 8
Forewarned is Forearmed

A wealth of archaeological information was unearthed during the previous century. At the turn of the century, literally tons of Koine Greek papyri were discovered in Egypt, shedding new light on the vocabulary, grammar, and style of the New Testament words. The middle of the century gave us the Dead Sea Scrolls and open access to ancient Jewish texts, such as the Mishna.[44] The end of the century brought with it the release of the cave four scrolls and scholarship into the early Jewish targums.[45]

From a geological perspective, this massive information dump has happened overnight. It's still going to take time for the bulk of information to make its way into translation lexicons, perhaps even a couple of decades.

It's interesting to observe how slowly information gets used, even when it finally does make its way into standard translation dictionaries. Take *A Greek-English Lexicon of the New Testament and Other Early Christian Literature* as an example. This Greek-to-English dictionary is often referred to as the BDAG. The first English edition appeared in 1957, the second in 1979, and the third in 2000. Now, are

44 The Mishna contains the sayings and opinions of the Jewish sages and rabbis from about 300 BCE to 220 CE.

45 Targums were books which contain the ancient interpretation of every verse of the Jewish scripture.

you ready for a surprise? The third edition boasts more than 15,000 new citations (primarily from finally including some Koine papyri and early Christian writings).

What's so surprising about that? *It took one hundred years for the discovered papyri to become part of this standard translation lexicon.*

And this still isn't the end of the story. Even after taking one hundred years for the information to finally be added, much of it still isn't being used in modern Bible translations.

Allow me to illustrate using Jesus' Sermon on the Mount as an example. At the moment, the most modern translation available is the New International Version (2011 edition). It was published eleven years after the BDAG finally added 15,000 citations. Now consider the first warning that Jesus gave after the sermon's surprising conclusion:

> Beware of the false prophets, who come to you in sheep's clothing, but inwardly are ravenous wolves. You will know them by their fruits. Grapes are not gathered from thorn bushes nor figs from thistles, are they?
>
> So every **good** tree bears **good** fruit, but the **bad** tree bears **bad** fruit. A **good** tree cannot produce **bad** fruit, nor can a **bad** tree produce **good** fruit. Every tree that does not bear **good** fruit is cut down and thrown into the fire.[46]

So, after Jesus' highly nuanced, very specific, earth-shattering statement, did he then shift into a generic "be good, not bad, or burn" message? Or is it possible that he uttered another highly nuanced, very specific, earth-shattering statement? One hundred years after the information was discovered, the BDAG finally says that this is so.

The BDAG says that the "good tree" means "useful tree."[47] It says that the "good fruit" is "useful fruit."[48] It says the "bad trees" is a reference to "plants and their products which are of inferior quality."[49] And it says the "bad fruit" is "so deficient in quality in a physical sense as to be worthless."[50]

---

46 Matthew 7:15-19 NIV (2011 Edition)
47 BDAG (2000 Edition) entry for *agathos*
48 BDAG (2000 Edition) entry for *kalos*
49 BDAG (2000 Edition) entry for *sapros*
50 BDAG (2000 Edition) entry for *poneros*

Where did the BDAG get these ideas? It got its translation from the Koine Greek papyri. So even if we used the BDAG straight up (without any additional investigation) we'd end up with a very nuanced outcome:

> So every **useful** tree bears **useful** fruit, but the **low quality** tree bears **worthless** fruit. A **useful** tree cannot produce **worthless** fruit, nor can a **low quality** tree produce **useful** fruit. Every tree that does not bear **useful** fruit is cut down and thrown into the fire.

Now does this translation, which is a plug and play from a standard lexicon, snap right on to Jesus' Sermon on the Mount? Yes, in a brilliant fashion. Jesus says that treating others the same way you want to be treated is the Law and the Prophets, the narrow road to life. And then he says to beware of religious people who do nothing to help others ("are worthless"). They will be chopped up and thrown into the fire. One idea seamlessly flows into another.

Even though the discovered Koine meanings significantly clarify the teachings of Jesus of Nazareth, modern Bibles still aren't using the meanings one hundred and eleven years after their discovery. Millions of Christians are relying on books that are demonstrably more than a century out of date. And this is another reason why the key to solving the Sermon on the Mount has taken so long to find.

Later in this book, I'll teach you a simple secret to bypass the information backlog. But for now, let's explore the final two warnings that Jesus gave at the end of his sermon:

> **Warning Number Two:**
>
> Not everyone who says to Me, 'Lord, Lord,' will enter the kingdom of heaven, but he who does the will of My Father who is in heaven will enter. Many will say to Me on that day, 'Lord, Lord, did we not prophesy in Your name, and in Your name cast out demons, and in Your name perform many miracles?'
>
> And then I will declare to them, 'I never knew you; DEPART FROM ME, YOU WHO PRACTICE LAWLESSNESS.'[51]

51 Matthew 7:21-23 NASB

Warning Number Three:

Therefore everyone who hears these words of Mine and acts on them, may be compared to a wise man who built his house on the rock. And the rain fell, and the floods came, and the winds blew and slammed against that house; and yet it did not fall, for it had been founded on the rock.

Everyone who hears these words of Mine and does not act on them, will be like a foolish man who built his house on the sand. The rain fell, and the floods came, and the winds blew and slammed against that house; and it fell--and great was its fall."[52]

The NASB Bible captures the last two warnings very well. However, it may be helpful to realize that 'those who practice lawlessness' refers to 'those who break the Law' (those who are Lawbreakers).

Now let's summarize the three warnings to simplify finding the key:

- Treat others the same way you want to be treated, for this is the Law.
    - The low quality trees bearing worthless fruit will be chopped up and thrown into the fire.
    - God will say, "Get away from me, you who broke the Law."
    - Everyone who hears these words and ignores them will be destroyed like a house built on sand during a storm.

So let's see what connects them all together.

- Treat others the same way you want to be treated, for this is the Law.
    - **Only those who actually follow this interpretation of the Law will make it on judgment day,** for the low quality trees bearing worthless fruit will be chopped up and thrown into the fire.
    - **Only those who actually follow this interpretation of the Law will make it on judgment day,** for God will say, "Get away from me you who broke the Law."
    - **Only those who actually follow this interpretation of the Law will make it on judgment day,** for everyone who hears

52 Matthew 7:24-27 NASB

> these words and ignores them will be destroyed like a house built on sand during a storm.

Jesus uttered the warnings to assure his readers that only those who follow *his* interpretation of the Law will make it on judgment day. This is the key to the warnings. This is the statement that encompasses them all. With it, we're finally able to piece together the structure of the entire Sermon on the Mount:

The Structure of Jesus'
Sermon on the Mount

I. **Beatitudes**: Jesus calls the crowds to gather around him.

II. **Introduction**: Jesus announces that he has come to give an interpretation of the Law and the Prophets that encompasses every commandment down to the smallest one.

III. **Body**: God is going to treat you based on how you treat others.

   a. *Only if you treat people better than the scribes and the Pharisees can you enter the kingdom of heaven.*

   b. *Your Father in heaven will reward you when you secretly give to the poor.*

   c. *God will forgive your sins in direct proportion to your forgiveness of others.*

   d. *You store up treasures in heaven by generously sharing with those in need.*

   e. *Don't worry about your own needs. Just focus on bringing God's kingdom to earth by expressing loving kindness and God will meet your needs as well.*

   f. *Whatever measure you use on others, God will use on you.*

   g. *Treat others well, because as a child of God, your heavenly Father will give you far greater rewards than you can possibly give even to your own family.*

IV. **Conclusion**: In everything, therefore, treat others the same way you want to be treated, for this is the Law and the Prophets, the narrow road to life. [This is the interpretation that encompasses all the commandments of scripture down to the smallest one.]

V. **Warnings**: Only those who actually follow this interpretation of the Law will make it on judgment day.

a. *The low quality trees bearing worthless fruit will be chopped up and thrown into the fire.*

b. *God will say, "Get away from me, you who broke the Law."*

c. *Everyone who hears these words of mine and ignores them will be destroyed like a house built on sand during a storm.*

Now that we've assembled the structure, we've found that the proposed key does encompass the entire sermon: *I have not come to abolish the Law and the Prophets because only the neighbor-based commands are the Law and the Prophets.* Every sentence from beginning to end contributes to this statement. *This* is the meaning of the Sermon on the Mount. The original meaning of the Sermon on the Mount has finally been solved.

This is the beauty of Biblical cryptanalysis. It takes a seemingly discombobulated list of teachings and finds the seamless thread that unifies them all. But the greatest beauty isn't found in the technical purity—it's in the real life implications. Can you imagine the impact this sermon had on the crowd? Jesus of Nazareth discarded one subset of their Law while leaving the other subset fully intact. (Jesus discarded the commands between man and God while leaving all the neighbor-based commands fully intact.) And the religious leaders were very upset.

Puzzle #2

The Gospel of Matthew

Chapter 9
Gemilut Chasadim

More than two centuries before Jesus was born, the Jewish sages had already made the legal distinction between 'that which is done for God' and 'that which is done for the neighbor':

> The world rests on three pillars: *Torah, avodah, gemilut chasadim.*—Shimon HaTzadik around 280 BCE[53]

- *Torah* originally referred to the study of the scriptures.
- *Avodah* had a dualistic meaning: work/worship. It expressed the devotional jobs done for God.
- *Gemilut chasadim* meant "performing acts of loving kindness."

Through the study of *torah,* a person learns *avodah* (devotional jobs done for God) and *gemilut chasadim* (acts of loving kindness done for others). The *torah* contained a number of required *gemilut chasadim* (acts of loving kindness done for others), such as feeding the hungry, sheltering the homeless, clothing the naked and visiting the sick.[54, 55]

53 Ethics of the Fathers 1:2 (an ancient Jewish writing)

54 *What the Rabbis Said: 250 Topics from the Talmud* By Ronald L. Eisenberg, p. 12

55 *Basic Judaism for Young People* Vol. 1, "Gemilut Chasadim," pp. 29-36

Keep in mind the concept and examples of *gemilut chasadim* as you read Jesus' quintessential teaching on judgment:

> But when the Son of Man comes in his majesty, and all the angels with him, then he will sit on his majestic throne. All the nations will be gathered before him and he will separate them from one another just as the shepherd separates the sheep from the goats. And he will place the sheep on his right and the goats on the left.
>
> Then the king will say to those on his right, "Come here! you who are blessed of my father, **take possession of the kingdom held for you from the foundation of the world because I was hungry and thirsty, and you gave me food and drink; I was a stranger and you invited me in; I was naked and you clothed me; I was sick and you visited me**; I was in prison and you came to me."
>
> Then those who treated people altruistically will reply to him, "Your highness, when did we see you hungry and feed you, or thirsty and give you something to drink? And when did we see you a stranger and invite you in, or naked and clothe you? When did we see you sick, or in prison, and come to visit you?"
>
> The king will answer saying to them, "I assure you that as much as you did it to one of these brothers of mine, the lowest in society, you did it to me."
>
> And then he will say to those on his left, "**Go away from me, accursed ones, into the fire of the age which has been held for the devil and his angels because I was hungry and you gave me nothing to eat; I was thirsty and you gave me nothing; I was a stranger and you did not invite me in; naked, and you did not clothe me; sick, and in prison, and you didn't visit me.**"
>
> Then they also will answer, "Your highness, when did we see you hungry, or thirsty, or a stranger, or naked, or sick, or in prison and did not be of service to you?'
>
> Then he will answer them saying, 'I assure you, as much as you didn't do it to the lowest of society, you didn't do it to me."
>
> These will go away into the punishment of the age, and those who treated others altruistically into the life of the age.[56]

56 Matthew 25:31-46

In this passage, Jesus used the all-important word, 'because'. He said that people inherit the kingdom *because of their gemilut chasadim*. In fact, he said that all humanity will be divided into two groups based solely on their *gemilut chasadim*. Like it or hate it, that's what he taught. And most of his fellow Jews hated it. After all, it flew in the face of centuries of tradition. It wasn't an easy message for them to embrace.

Jesus' two most famous discourses are his Sermon on the Mount and his quintessential teaching on judgment. The entire Sermon on the Mount was devoted to teaching that only the neighbor-based commandments are the Law (the commandments between man and God are not). And the quintessential teaching on judgment taught that only *gemilut chasadim* will matter on judgment day (and *avodah* [devoted jobs done for God] will not). They are both teaching the very same thing in their own particular way.

But how could Jesus say all this? Was he a heretic? Didn't he believe in serving God? We'll find Matthew's answer to all three of these questions in the following chapter.

Chapter 10
Just One Way

In first century Judea, the annual Day of Atonement was the most sacred holiday. This was the day that the Jewish nation believed they could find forgiveness for all the sins they had committed.[57] Only through the forgiveness of sins could they be reconciled to God and inherit life in his kingdom.

On the Day of Atonement, an animal sacrifice was necessary for the forgiveness of sins.[58] Animal sacrifice was the only way to repair the transgressions they had committed against God.[59] Keep this in mind as you read the following:

> Then it happened that as Jesus was reclining at the table in the house, behold, many tax collectors and sinners came and were dining with Jesus and His disciples.
>
> When the Pharisees saw this, they said to His disciples, "Why is your Teacher eating with the tax collectors and sinners?"
>
> But when Jesus heard this, He said, "It is not those who are healthy who need a physician, but those who are sick. **But go and learn what this means: 'I DESIRE COMPASSION, AND NOT SACRIFICE,'** for I did not come to call the righteous, but sinners."[60]

57 Mishna Yoma 8:9 (an ancient Jewish writing)

58 Leviticus 16:29-30; 23:27-31; Numbers 29:7

59 Mishna Yoma 8:9 (an ancient Jewish writing)

60 Matthew 9:10-13 NASB

From a first century Jewish perspective, there's a whole lot of subtext going on here. First, Jesus rebukes the religious leaders and criticizes them for not understanding a prophet from their own scriptures. Ouch.

Second, his criticism struck at the very heart of the Jewish religion: the forgiveness of sins. He was saying the religious leaders didn't understand the correct way to repair man's transgressions against God. Double ouch.

Before we discuss the third and final blow, let's dig a little deeper into the word that is translated as "compassion." Let's find out the first century understanding of that word—because it's going to surprise you.

When Jesus said, "I desire compassion and not sacrifice," he was quoting the prophet Hosea, a prophet from the Jewish scriptures. In first century Judea, most Jews used a Greek version of the scriptures called the Septuagint. But the Pharisaic writings and Dead Sea Scrolls show that the religious leaders continually maintained an awareness of the Hebrew words underlying the Greek translation. Can you guess what Hebrew word was translated as "compassion" in the Hosea quote? If you guessed that it was based on *chasadim,*[61] then give yourself a gold star.

So now, for the third and final blow: Jesus showed that the prophet Hosea declared, *God wants loving kindness shown to others for the forgiveness of sins, not a sacrifice.* According to Hosea, *gemilut chasadim* (acts of loving kindness) repairs man's transgressions against God … and animal sacrifice does not. Uh oh, Toto, we're not in Kansas anymore.

So yes, Jesus believed in serving God. It's because he believed in serving God that he wanted everyone to follow God's only method for the forgiveness of sins: *gemilut chasadim* (acts of loving kindness, treating others the same way that you want to be treated). Now we know the theological basis of both his Sermon on the Mount and his

61 Literally: *chesed*, which means loving kindness. *Gemilut chasadim* are 'acts of *chesed*,' i.e. 'acts of loving kindness.'

quintessential teaching on judgment. Now we know that he really meant what he said in both of them.

Chapter 11
Ten Commandments on a Diet

We're discovering how important it is to understand the ancient grouping of the Law into two distinct subsets, for Jesus' teachings on salvation and judgment are composed around them. They are composed to show that only the neighbor-based commands will matter on judgment day (and that the commands between man and God won't matter at all). So how did this ancient grouping into two distinct subsets even begin? It goes all the way back to Moses and his famous Ten Commandments.

The ancients noticed that the Ten Commandments were already grouped into two subsets. The first four ordinances were based on a devoted love of God, and the remaining ones were based on loving our neighbors as ourselves.

For example, the first four commandments were:

The Ten Commandments
Love God with all your being

1. You shall have no other gods before me

2. You shall not make for yourself an idol

3. Do not take the name of the Lord in vain

4. Remember the Sabbath and keep it holy

And the remaining commandments were:

The Ten Commandments
Love your neighbor as yourself

5. Honor your father and mother
6. You shall not murder
7. You shall not commit adultery
8. You shall not steal
9. You shall not tell falsehoods about your neighbor
10. You shall not covet anything that belongs to your neighbor

This foundational code was divided into 'commands between man and God' and 'commands between man and neighbor.' So the Jews followed suit with all the other hundreds of commands found in scripture. And since the 'commands between man and God' came first in Moses' list, the Jews naturally considered these to be the most important ones.

With this in mind, think how provocative the following passage must've been to its original first century Jewish audience:

> And someone came to him and said, "Teacher, which beneficient thing must I do that I may have the life of the age to come?"
>
> But he answered him, "Why are you asking me about what is beneficient. There is only one who is beneficient. **But if you want to enter into that life, keep the commandments."**
>
> **The man said to him, "Which kind?"**
>
> **And Jesus said, "Don't murder, don't be unfaithful, don't steal, don't lie, honor your father and mother—love your neighbor as yourself."**[62]

When the man asked which kind of commandments he must follow to inherit life in the age to come, did Jesus say, "Both kinds"? No, he did not. When the man asked which kind of commandments he must follow to inherit life in the age to come, did Jesus say, "None

62 Matthew 19:16-19

of them"? No, he did not. When the man asked which kind of commandments he must follow to inherit life in the age to come, Jesus said, "Those that are based on loving your neighbor as yourself." And he did so in a dramatic fashion at that.

Let me remind you which ordinances from the Ten Commandments are based on loving your neighbor:

5. **Honor your father and mother**
6. **You shall not murder**
7. **You shall not commit adultery**
8. **You shall not steal**
9. **You shall not tell falsehoods about your neighbor**
10. You shall not covet anything that belongs to your neighbor

Jesus called out the first five by name to give his examples of "which kind." Then, just to make sure the man got his point, he unequivocally declared that it is the kind of commandments based on loving your neighbor as yourself. Could there be any clearer teaching in which Jesus discarded the commands between man and God, leaving only the neighbor-based commands fully intact? Jesus jumped right over the big four when he gave his examples. He jumped right over the four foundational commandments between man and God.

But what about the first four commandments? How could he just jump right over them?

Chapter 12
Trump Card

Doing absolutely no work whatsoever (such as harvesting food) on the Sabbath was one of the four commands between man and God in Moses' Ten Commandments:

1. You shall have no other gods before me
2. You shall not make for yourself an idol
3. Do not take the name of the Lord in vain
4. **Remember the Sabbath and keep it holy**

Moses' Law clarifies that this means no work *at all.* In fact, Moses' Law required the Jews to stone a man to death for gathering wood on the Sabbath (perhaps to keep his family warm).[63] The zero work policy really meant *zero work.*

With this in mind, let's take a look at the following passage:

> At that time Jesus went through the grainfields on the Sabbath, and His disciples became hungry and began to pick the heads of grain and eat.
>
> But when the Pharisees saw this, they said to Him, "Look, **Your disciples do what is not lawful to do on a Sabbath.**"
>
> But He said to them, "Have you not read what David did when he became hungry, he and his companions, how he entered the house of God, and they

63 Numbers 15:32-36

> ate the consecrated bread, which was not lawful for him to eat nor for those with him, but for the priests alone? Or have you not read in the Law, that on the Sabbath the priests in the temple break the Sabbath and are innocent? But I say to you that something greater than the temple is here. **But if you had known what this means, 'I DESIRE COMPASSION, AND NOT A SACRIFICE,' you would not have condemned the innocent.**[64]

Ah, Jesus pulled out the Hosea card, forcing the Pharisees to drop any stones that they might've picked up. After all, they couldn't cast any stones unless they could rebut Jesus' scriptural response.

As a reminder, the Hosea passage says that people repair their broken relationship to God through loving kindness shown to others. Since Jesus and his disciples were the epitome of loving kindness, all their transgressions against God were covered—even their violation of the Sabbath. Had the Pharisees understood Hosea's words, they wouldn't have condemned *the innocent* (those whose sins were already washed as white as snow by their acts of loving kindness).

Now we know why the neighbor-based commands were all that mattered to Jesus. For as long as a person loves his neighbor as himself, he has availed himself of God's one way to repair all his transgressions against God. This includes every transgression against God, even violation of the big four.

64 Matthew 12:1-7 NASB

Chapter 13
The Final Countdown

The religious leaders of Jesus' day were in a pickle. Anytime they accused Jesus of breaking any Law, bam! Out came the Hosea card. What a dreadful inconvenience. "What to do, what to do, what to do," they must've pondered. Then suddenly, a religious expert in the Law figured that he knew exactly what to do … he thought he had found a way to shut Jesus up once and for all. Jesus was going to be toast.

The first four books of the Jewish scriptures (the Pentateuch) were considered to be the very foundation of Jewish Law. These books trumped the Prophets. After all, the Prophets were based on them, not the other way around. The lawyer figured that he could use the Pentateuch to squash Jesus' teachings once and for all. Bye bye, Hosea trump card.

The most important commandment in the entire Pentateuch was: *Love the Lord your God with all your heart, body, soul, and strength.* In fact, the Jews wore jewelry which housed little scrolls with these words written on them. This jewelry, called phylacteries, was tied to the forehead and hands of all first century Jews in obedience to the following scripture:

> **You shall love the LORD your God with all your heart and with all your soul and with all your might. These words**, which I am commanding you today, shall be on your heart. You shall teach them diligently to your sons and shall talk of them when you sit in your house and when you walk by the

> way and when you lie down and when you rise up. **You shall bind them as a sign on your hand and they shall be as frontals on your forehead.**[65]

Now the phylacteries worn by the Pharisees weren't tiny little trinkets. Quite the opposite. The Pharisees supersized them:

> But they do all their works to be noticed by men. For **they widen their phylacteries** and lengthen the tassels of their garments.[66]

The Pharisees' phylacteries, containing the greatest commandment in the Law, were billboards designed for everyone to see.

So everywhere people went, they saw phylacteries big and small dangling from Jewish hands and foreheads. All day long, innumerable copies of the greatest commandment danced around first century Judea. With this in mind, consider how the following passage is translated in the NASB Bible:

> But when the Pharisees heard that Jesus had silenced the Sadducees, they gathered themselves together. One of them, a lawyer, asked Him a question, **testing Him**, "Teacher, which is the great commandment in the Law?"[67]

Excuse me? The lawyer was testing to see if Jesus might possibly be familiar with the one commandment that they all had dangling from their foreheads and hands? Clearly, something else was going on here. The lawyer wasn't testing Jesus; the lawyer was trapping Jesus. The lawyer (possibly even dangling one of his supersized phylacteries in Jesus' face) asked the question, knowing Jesus' response in advance. The lawyer believed that Jesus would be forced to retract his statement that: *You only need to follow the kind of commandments based on love of neighbor to inherit life in the age to come.*

> But when the Pharisees heard that Jesus had silenced the Sadducees, they got together in a group. One of them, an expert in the Law, asked Jesus a question **to trap him**. "Teacher, what is the great commandment in the Law?"

So did Jesus retract his teaching that only the neighbor-based commands are the Law? Did Jesus retract every single teaching on

65 Deuteronomy 6:5-8
66 Matthew 23:5 NASB
67 Matthew 22:34-36 NASB

judgment and salvation recorded in the rest of the Gospel of Matthew? If you read today's popular translations, you'd certainly come to that conclusion. But is this really what happened?

To understand Jesus' answer, we need to understand a little more about the group he was addressing … the Pharisees. One of the most popular (and universally respected) Pharisaic schools during Jesus' day was the School of Hillel.[68] Its founder had established seven rules for scripture interpretation.[69, 70] One of these rules was *G'zerah Shavah* which was based on equivalent expressions. According to this rule, any two scriptures, which use equivalent words or phrases, are cut from the same block—they are inextricably tied one to the other.[71]

Now, with this in mind, let's take a look at Jesus' response:

> And Jesus said to him, "'**You shall love** the Master your God with all your heart, and with all your soul, and with all your mind.' This is the great and first commandment. And the second is the same as it.[72] '**You shall love** your neighbor as yourself.' The whole Law hangs on both of these commandments unified together."

Jesus used *G'zerah Shavah* to show that "loving your neighbor" is the same as "loving God with your whole being." In other words, he used *G'zerah Shavah* to show that "loving your neighbor" entirely fulfills the command to "love God with your whole being." Since he used the Pharisees' own method of scripture interpretation, they had no comeback. And that was the end of the discussion.

It's important to note that the command to "love your neighbor as yourself" is also found in the Pentateuch. Therefore, Jesus used *G'zerah Shavah* on two Pentateuch commands, proving that only the neighbor-based commands *are the Law*. We have already seen that Jesus used the prophet Hosea to prove that only the neighbor-

68 *The Jewish Encyclopedia*, entry for HILLEL

69 t. Sanhedrin 7.11 (an ancient Jewish writing) details Hillel's seven rules including *G'zerah Shavah*

70 *Meet the Rabbis: Rabbinic Thought and the Teachings of Jesus* by Brad H. Young, p. 165

71 *Meet the Rabbis: Rabbinic Thought and the Teachings of Jesus* by Brad H. Young, pp. 165-167

72 Koine Greek: *homoia*. *Homoia* expressed a wide range of degrees of similarity all the way up to total sameness. The meaning of the word was understood relative to the context. In Jesus' use of *G'zerah Shavah* in the defense of his prior teachings, everyone present understood the sameness being referenced. And since Jesus used an accepted form of scripture interpretation, no one challenged his statement any further.

based commands *are the Prophets.* And now, we know why Jesus so confidently declared on the Mount of Olives:

> Treat others the same way you want to be treated for **this is the Law and the Prophets**.

When Jesus ascended the Mount of Olives, he promised to give an interpretation of scripture that didn't annul a single commandment, even down to the smallest one. Then he pulled a surprise; his entire interpretation says that only the neighbor-based commands are the Law and the Prophets. The rest of the book of Matthew shows how Jesus proved his point. Through Hosea, he showed that this was the Prophets. And by applying *G'zerah Shavah* to the Pentateuch, he proved this was the Law. So yes, the entire book of Matthew was written to convey a single teaching: *Jesus did not come to abolish the Law and the Prophets because only the neighbor-based commands are the Law and the Prophets.*

"But wait!" you may protest. "Did the earliest Jewish Christians understand the connection? Did they really understand that, because of *G'zerah Shavah*, the Golden Rule totally fulfills *both* the love of God *and* neighbor?"

Chapter 14
The Didache

One of the earliest Jewish Christian documents in existence is the *Didache* (also called *The Teaching of the Twelve Apostles*). According to the *Oxford Dictionary of the Christian Church*, most scholars place the date of authorship at some point between the mid- to late first century.[73] There have been many English translations of it since its discovery in 1873. However, no translation of the *Didache* even begins to approach the level of detail as that of Aaron Milavec's translation.

Milavec's passion to express the details of the Didache led him to adopt a systematic form of English notation. Where a single Greek word had to be translated using multiple English words, Milavec linked the multiple words together with underlined characters (so the reader would know that the multiple words come from a single Greek word). Since Greek distinguishes between the singular and plural, Milavec placed an umlaut above the first vowel in the English word to signify that the Greek specified the plural. (For example: "präy" would indicate that the underlying Greek was telling multiple people to pray; whereas "pray" would indicate that the underlying Greek was telling one person to pray.) And so on, and so on.

The end result was that every Greek word was ultimately reflected in the translation. At first, you may wonder why such stringency is so important. Let me give you an example of how

73 *Oxford Dictionary of the Christian Church* (2005 Edition): Didache

important Milavec's penchant for detail turned out to be. Below are the second and third sentences of the *Didache* in its original Koine Greek:

> Ἡ μὲν οὖν τῆς ζωῆς ἐστιν αὕτη· πρῶτον ἀγαπησεις τὸν θεὸν τὸν ποιήσαντά σε, δεύτερον τὸν πλησίον σου ὡς σεαυτόν· πάντα δὲ ὅσα ἐὰν θελήσῃς μὴ γίνεσθαί σοι, καὶ σὺ ἄλλῳ μὴ ποίει.

I provided the Koine text above because most English translations skip right over the second word μὲν. But in Milavec's case, every word is dutifully reflected in the translation, allowing the reader to understand many important details regarding the text.[74]

So what's so important about the word *μὲν*? This word was a marker of correlation. It often was used to express two identical concepts: on one hand/on the other hand,[75] one side of the coin/the other side of the coin. The Didache used the word to correlate the following two concepts:

> **On one side of the coin, the way of life is this:** Firstly, you will love God who made you, and secondly, you will love your neighbor as yourself.
>
> **The other side of the same coin is this:** Whatever you do not want to happen to you, likewise don't do to another.

That's right. The earliest Christian Jews understood that the Golden Rule encompasses *both* the love of God and the love of neighbor. The earliest Christians must've understood that the second commandment, "love of neighbor," is the total fulfillment of the first, "love God," for that's the only way the Golden Rule could possibly encompass them both. So we see that the early Jewish Christians fully understood Jesus' use of equivalent expressions when he was confronted to explain the greatest commandment of the Law. We see that they understood his response to be the mirror image of the Golden Rule.

---

74 See *The Didache: Text, Translation, Analysis, and Commentary* By Aaron Milavec pages 2-3.

75 *A Greek-English Lexicon of the New Testament and Other Early Christian Literature*, 3rd Edition, entry for *μὲν*

Chapter 15
Jesus in a Nutshell

Now that we understand what Jesus taught in the Gospel of Matthew from a first century Jewish perspective, we are ready to solve the second puzzle. We are ready to find the key that encompasses all of Jesus' teachings on salvation and judgment found in the Gospel of Matthew:

Jesus' Teachings in Matthew

- Treat others the same way you want to be treated, for this is the Law and the Prophets.
- People will inherit the kingdom because of their acts of loving kindness.
- God desires loving kindness shown to others, not animal sacrifice, for the forgiveness of sins.
- If you want to inherit life in the coming age, follow all the commandments based on loving your neighbor as yourself.
- By fulfilling the command to love your neighbor as yourself, you are fulfilling the command to love God with your whole being.

Jesus' teachings on salvation and judgment are his essential teachings. They are the ones that show what Jesus considered to be the deciding factor on who gets the punishment and who gets the reward. So now, as far as Jesus' essential teachings in Matthew are concerned, we have an important key to solve. We must identify a single statement that encompasses all the Matthew teachings.

The cryptanalytic solution is given below:

The Key to
Jesus' Teachings in Matthew

- **I have not come to abolish the Law and the Prophets because only the neighbor-based commands are the Law and the Prophets.** Therefore, treating others the same way you want to be treated is the Law and the Prophets.

- **I have not come to abolish the Law and the Prophets because only the neighbor-based commands are the Law and the Prophets.** Therefore, people will inherit the kingdom because of their acts of loving kindness.

- **I have not come to abolish the Law and the Prophets because only the neighbor-based commands are the Law and the Prophets.** Therefore, God desires loving kindness shown to others, not animal sacrifice, for the forgiveness of sins.

- **I have not come to abolish the Law and the Prophets because only the neighbor-based commands are the Law and the Prophets.** Therefore, if you want to inherit life in the coming age, follow all the commandments based on loving your neighbor as yourself.

- **I have not come to abolish the Law and the Prophets because only the neighbor-based commands are the Law and the Prophets.** Therefore, by fulfilling the command to love your neighbor as yourself, you are fulfilling the command to love God with your whole being.

We have succeeded in the Biblical cryptanalysis of Matthew. We have successfully found the single statement that explains all of Jesus' essential teachings—his teachings regarding salvation and judgment as recorded in the Gospel of Matthew. And look! The key to Jesus' Sermon on the Mount is the key to all of Jesus' essential teachings on salvation and judgment in the Gospel of Matthew.

So now we understand the revolutionary teaching that started it all. The dual division of the Law permeated the first century Judaic culture. Their religious vocabulary pivoted around the division. They even wore jewelry containing the command to love God in order to remind them of which division of the Law was the most important. And then, Jesus came along.

Jesus of Nazareth discarded the seemingly most important subset of the Law, while leaving the other subset fully intact. Jesus discarded all the devotional jobs done for God, while leaving the neighbor-based commands fully intact. This was the revolutionary message that rocked first century Judea.

The second puzzle—the Gospel of Matthew—has been solved.

"But wait!" the critic may protest once again. "That's just Matthew. What about the other Gospels: Mark, Luke, and John? Certainly, such a teaching is inconsistent with their version of Jesus' lessons. Certainly, they didn't teach that salvation comes solely from loving our neighbors as ourselves."

First, let's be clear. We've laid sufficient groundwork to show that this was the consistent teaching of Matthew's Jesus. But the critic still has a valid concern. After all, many atheists charge the Bible with being highly inconsistent. So, are Mark, Luke, and John's version of Jesus' teachings consistent with Matthew's? Let's find out.

Chapter 16
Three Couples

The first five books of the New Testament are: Matthew, Mark, Luke, John, and Acts. It's natural to wonder how the new discoveries regarding Matthew are related to the other four books. There is a rule of interpretation that is of great help in finding out. And that is 'The Three Couples Rule':

> **Three Couples Rule**
>
> There are three natural couples (Biblical books to be interpreted together as a pair): Matthew/Mark, Luke/Acts, John/1 John.

Allow me to explain.

The Gospel of Matthew contains almost the entire Gospel of Mark inside it. In fact, 612 of the 662 verses in Mark are also found in Matthew, mostly in the same order. In general, Matthew expands upon the teachings found in Mark, providing additional explanation of what he wrote. Occasionally, however, Mark adds a detail that is not covered in Matthew. Matthew and Mark are best interpreted together, as a couple. This will avoid the problem of interpreting one in a manner that contradicts the other.

Many people note the absence of theology in the book of Acts. It is a historical book written by the same author as the Gospel of Luke. The author lays out Jesus' theology in his gospel, and then explains how this gospel spread via his historical book. The best way to understand the occasional salvation terminology in Acts is by examining the theological basis for the terms in Luke. Luke and Acts are best interpreted together, as a couple.

And then, there's the famous Gospel of John, the favorite among modern denominations. We are fortunate that the Bible contains a letter from the same author (1 John). 1 John explains a lot of the terminology and doctrines found in the Gospel of John. Thus, the Gospel of John and 1 John are best interpreted together, as a couple. This will avoid the problem of interpreting one in a manner that contradicts the other.

So let's explore the application of the key to the three couples.

Let's begin with the Matthew/Mark pair.

Matthew:

> But when the Pharisees heard that Jesus had silenced the Sadducees, they got together in a group. One of them, an expert in the Law, asked Jesus a question to trap him. "Teacher, what is the great commandment in the Law?"
>
> And Jesus said to him, **"'You shall love the Lord your God with all your heart, and with all your soul, and with all your mind.' This is the great and first commandment. And the second is the same as it.**[76] **'You shall love your neighbor as yourself.'"**
>
> * * *
>
> But if you had known what this means, '**I desire loving kindness, not a sacrifice**,' you wouldn't have condemned the innocent.[77]
>
> * * *
>
> But when Jesus overheard this he said, "It's not the healthy who need a healer, but those who are ill. But go and learn what this means, '**I desire loving kindness, not a sacrifice.**'" Because I

76 Koine Greek: *homoia*. *Homoia* expressed a wide range of degrees of similarity all the way up to total sameness. The meaning of the word was understood relative to the context. In Jesus' use of *G'zerah Shavah* in the defense of his prior teachings, everyone present understood the sameness being referenced. And since Jesus used an accepted form of scripture interpretation, no one challenged his statement any further.

77 Matthew 12:7

didn't come to call those who treat others equitably but those who have missed the mark.[78]

Mark:

An expert in religious commandments came by and heard their debates. And observing that Jesus had answered them commendably, he asked him, "What commandment is the foremost of them all?"

Jesus answered, "The foremost is, 'Hear O Israel, the Lord our God is one Lord; and you shall love the Lord your God with all your heart, and with all your soul, and with all your mind, and with all your strength.' And the second is the same as it,[79] "You shall love your neighbor as yourself." There is no other commandment greater than these.

The scribe said to him, "Right, teacher, you have spoken the truth. He is one and there is no one else beside him, and to love him with all the heart and with all the mind and with all the strength. And to love your neighbor as yourself is much more than all the burnt offerings and sacrifices."

When Jesus saw he answered with understanding, he said to him, "You are close to entering the Kingdom of God." After that, no one would venture to ask him any more questions.

The Gospel of Mark passage ends with a strong statement, "After that, no one would venture to ask him any more questions." *Mark paints this as Jesus' defining moment.* This is the moment in Mark where Jesus declares his theology and simultaneously silences his critics. This is the moment in Mark where Jesus declares: *Only the neighbor-based commands are the Law and the Prophets ... and proves it at the same time.*

Huh? Where is all of that? Mark's Gospel was also written to a first century Jewish audience. His original audience was intimately familiar with the School of Hillel's seven rules of scripture interpretation. They were all intimately familiar with the *G'zerah Shavah* rule. As a

78 Matthew 9:13

79 Both the Byzantine Majority Text and the Textus Receptus have *homoia* in Mark 12:31. But modern committees removed this word from the verse when creating the Critical Text. Yet the scribe's response doesn't make sense without this word, which shows that the word was indeed in the original manuscript (as both the Byzantine Majority Text and the Textus Repectus attest).

reminder, any scriptures that shared equivalent words or expressions were isolated (independent of surrounding context), then fused together under the assumption that they were 'cut from the same block.' While such a rule is foreign, if not anathema, to modern scholars ... the original text cannot be understood independent of the audience to which it was written. The text was structured to communicate a message to *them*. We have to know *their* mindset to understand the message in the first place.

So here's how the exchange went down from a bird's eye view. First, Jesus uses equivalent expressions to show that the love of neighbor is the total fulfillment of the greatest commandment *in the Law*. Then the scribe shows he understands the *G'zerah Shavah* by declaring that the love of neighbor is the total fulfillment of the greatest commandment *in the Prophets*. "After that, no one would venture to ask him any more questions." And how could they? Once they understood that the neighbor-based commands were the entire Law and the Prophets—the entire canonical scripture—the case was closed.

Notice that Mark states that *the scribe understood Jesus' point.*

> When Jesus saw he answered with understanding...

So what exactly did the scribe understand?

> The scribe said to him, "Right, teacher, you have spoken the truth. He is one and there is no one else beside him, and to love him with all the heart and with all the mind and with all the strength. And to love your neighbor as yourself is much more than all the burnt offerings and sacrifices."

The scribe understood that love of God is the greatest commandment, and he understood that love of neighbor (not animal sacrifices) is what fulfills it.

Did you happen to notice that the scribe's response is based on Jesus' favorite Hosea quote?

> I desire loving kindness and not a sacrifice.[80]

80 Hosea 6:6

So Jesus used *G'zerah Shavah* on the Pentateuch to prove love of neighbor fulfills the entire Law. And the scribe demonstrates his understanding by showing love of neighbor fulfills the greatest commandment according to the Prophets.

Matthew expounded upon Mark's version. In the Sermon on the Mount, Matthew shows Jesus explicitly stating that the neighbor-based commands are the Law and the Prophets (something that Mark showed through example, not statement). Matthew shows Jesus explicitly stating that this is the complete interpretation of the Law and the Prophets, down to the smallest commandment (something that Mark showed through example, not statement). Matthew separates Jesus' proof that this is the entire Law from his proof that this is the entire Prophets (something Mark deals with in one fell swoop). While Matthew's divide-and-conquer approach is much easier to digest, make no mistake about it: Matthew and Mark taught the exact same thing.

Let's take a look at another Matthew/Mark pair:

Matthew:

> And someone came to him and said, "Teacher, which beneficient thing must I do that I may have the life of the age to come?"
>
> But he answered him, "Why are you asking me about what is beneficient. There is only one who is beneficient. But if you want to enter into that life, keep the commandments."
>
> The man said to him, "Which kind?"
>
> And Jesus said, "**Don't murder, don't be unfaithful, don't steal, don't lie, honor your father and mother—love your neighbor as yourself.**"
>
> The young man said to him, "I have kept all these things, what am I still lacking?"
>
> Jesus said to him, "If you want to be complete, go and sell your possessions and give to the poor, and you will have treasure in heaven. Then come follow me."

> But when the young man heard this, he went away grieving, for he owned a lot of property.

Mark:

> As he was journeying, a man ran up and knelt down before him, and asked him, "Beneficent teacher, what shall I do to inherit the life of the age to come?"
>
> And Jesus said to him, "Why do you call me beneficent? No one is beneficent except God alone. You know the commandments: **Don't murder, don't be unfaithful, don't steal, don't lie, don't defraud, honor your father and mother**."
>
> And he said to him, "Teacher I have kept all these things since I was a child."
>
> Looking at him Jesus loved him and said, "There is something you lack. Go away and sell all your possessions and give to the poor, and you will have treasure in heaven. Then come, follow me.
>
> Because of these words he was dismayed, and he went away grief stricken, for he owned a lot of property.

Once again, Matthew explicitly states what Mark demonstrates by way of example. Matthew has Jesus explicitly stating that the only way to inherit the life of the age to come is by keeping the commandments (something that Mark demonstrates by way of example). Matthew also has Jesus explicitly stating that he's talking about every commandment related to "loving your neighbor as yourself" (something that Mark demonstrates by way of example).

Now, it's important to understand the Jewish context of: Go and sell all that you have and give to the poor, then come and follow me. Jesus wouldn't have declared the former without the latter. Jesus invited the man to be his disciple. The man's basic needs would be met via the discipleship relationship. The point wasn't to make the man destitute. Rather, the point was for the man not to hold onto anything extra, for if the needs of others are *completely* equal to your own, then one couldn't hold onto anything extra. This is what the man was lacking. This is what the man needed to do to be *complete*.

Anyone who loves his neighbor *as himself* could not hold onto anything extra. This concept explains our next pair: Luke/Acts

Luke:

> **Bear fruits corresponding to repentance** and don't begin to say to yourselves, "We have Abraham for our Father. For I tell you that from these stones God could raise up children to Abraham, and the axe is already laid at the root of the trees. Therefore every tree that does not bear exceptional fruit is cut down and thrown into the fire."
>
> And the crowds were questioning him saying, "Therefore what should we do?"
>
> And he answered them saying, "**The man who has two shirts is to share with him who has none. And he who has food is to do likewise.**"

Acts:

> But I, Paul, continued declaring both to those in Damascus (first), and Jerusalem, and throughout all the districts of Judea, and to the Gentiles, that they should repent and turn to God, performing **deeds corresponding to repentance.**

The Koine Greek phrase for 'corresponding to repentance' is *axia tes metanoia*. When people read the book of Acts, it's normal for them to wonder, "What exactly are these deeds that correspond to repentance?" All one has to do is look to Luke, which uses the same phrase. Luke's list of deeds "corresponding to repentance" begins with sharing your extras with those in need. Luke's list of deeds corresponding to repentance is based on loving your neighbor as yourself. *This* is the basis of repentance in Luke, and *this* is the basis of repentance in his other work: Acts.

Repentance in Acts bears no resemblance to what modern theologians say it means. They interpret Acts in a way that contradicts what the same author wrote in his other work. Luke's 'acts corresponding to repentance' are based on the premise that only the neighbor-based commands are the Law; so repent and follow them.

Let's examine another Luke/Acts pair:

Luke:

> And behold a lawyer stood up to entrap him saying, "Teacher, **what must I do to inherit the life** of the age to come?"
>
> And he said to him, "What is written in the Law? How does it read?"
>
> And he answered, "You shall love the Lord your God will all your heart, and with all your soul, and with all your strength, and with all your mind—**and your neighbor as yourself.**"
>
> **At this point Jesus said to him, "You have answered correctly. Do *this* and you will live."**
>
> **But wishing to vindicate himself, he said to Jesus, "And who is my neighbor?"**

Acts:

> On hearing this they calmed down and praised God saying, "So then God has given the Gentiles also **the repentance to life**.

Many translations of Luke gloss over the fact that Jesus singles out the command, "love your neighbor as yourself." Yet look at the lawyer's response. He knew exactly what Jesus was singling out. He got Jesus' point. The repentance to life is based on loving your neighbor as yourself. Do *this* and you will live.

But there's more to Luke's story … much more. The rest of the story drives home the point that only the neighbor-based commands are the Law, and the commands between man and God are not. But first, before we dive into the rest of the story, we need to understand first century Jewish culture (are you sensing a theme here?).

Although Jewish Law contained hundreds of commandments, the foundation of the Law was Moses' Ten Commandments. The first four commandments were the big four—they were the commandments between man and God:

Ten Commandments

(Between Man and God)

1. You shall have no other gods before me
2. You shall not make for yourself an idol
3. **Do not take the name of the Lord in vain**
4. **Remember the Sabbath and keep it holy**

The Jews' fierce enemies were the Samaritans. The Jews refused to pronounce God's name (in observance of the third commandment). But the Samaritans had the audacity to pronounce God's name.[81] And the Samaritans observed the Sabbath in a different way than the Jews, thereby making them (from a Jewish perspective) Sabbath breakers.[82] The heretical Samaritans violated two out of the four greatest commandments between man and God (and they violated other commandments between man and God, as well).

The Jews forbade intermarriage with Samaritans. They even forbade eating with them. *The Samaritans didn't keep the commandments between man and God, so they cannot inherit the life of the age to come.* Now, with this in mind, let's explore the whole story:

> And behold a lawyer stood up to entrap him saying, "Teacher, **what must I do to inherit the life** of the age to come?"
>
> And he said to him, "What is written in the Law? How does it read?"
>
> And he answered, "You shall love the Lord your God will all your heart, and with all your soul, and with all your strength, and with all your mind—**and your neighbor as yourself.**"
>
> **At this point Jesus said to him, "You have answered correctly. Do *this* and you will live."**
>
> **But wishing to vindicate himself, he said to Jesus, "And who is my neighbor?"**
>
> Jesus replied and said, "A man was coming from Jerusalem heading to

81 *The international standard Bible encyclopedia* by Geoffrey W. Bromiley, p. 307

82 Ant. 1 1.346 by Josephus (first century Jewish historian)

> Jericho and fell into the hands of robbers, who stripped him and beat him and left him half dead. By chance a priest came down that same road, and when he saw him he passed by the opposite side. In the same way also a Levite, when he approached the place and saw him, he passed by the other side.
>
> "But when a Samaritan on a journey came by and saw him, he empathized with him. And he went over to him and bandaged his wounds (pouring oil and wine on them) and he put him on his own animal, and brought him to an inn and took care of him. The next day he gave the inn keeper two denarii and said, "Take care of him. And whatever you spend in addition I will repay you when I return."
>
> "Which of the three do you suppose performed as a neighbor to the man who fell into the robbers hands?"
>
> And he said to him, "The one who showed **loving kindness**[83] to him."
>
> Then Jesus said to him, "Go and do the same."

This parable was Luke's way of discarding the commandments between man and God while leaving the neighbor-based commands fully intact. How so? Priests and Levites were the only two Jewish castes involved in temple service. They epitomized the link between man and God. However, these archetypes of observing the commands between man and God were not the ones who inherited life. On the contrary, a heretic known for breaking the commandments between man and God observed the Golden Rule, and received salvation because of it.

Now to complete our survey, let's take a look at the John/1 John pair.

1 John:

> Beloved, let us love one another, for love is from God; and **everyone who loves is born of God** and knows God. - NASB

John:

> Jesus answered and said to him, "Truly, truly, I say to you, **unless one is born again he cannot see the kingdom of God.**" - NASB

83 Jesus used the same Greek word here as is found in his favorite Isaiah quote, "I desire **loving kindness**, not a sacrifice.

Reading the Bible is easy, so long as you employ The Three Couples Rule. Anyone who loves his brother is born again and will inherit the kingdom of God as a result. That's John's own description of what Jesus taught in the Gospel that he wrote. What more can be said?

And finally, one more:

1 John:

> This is God's commandment: to **believe in the name of His Son Jesus Christ and therefore love one another**, just as he commanded us.

John:

> For God so loved the world, that he gave his only son, that **whoever believes in him shall not perish** but have life in the age to come.

Again, The Three Couples Rule makes reading the Bible a cinch. John interpreted 'to believe in Jesus' to mean 'trust him enough to do what he said'—trust him enough to love one another, just as he commanded us. Now we see why it's a good idea to allow John to interpret his own Gospel.

So yes, all the Gospels (Matthew, Mark, Luke, and John) taught the very same thing: *Jesus didn't come to abolish the Law and the Prophets because only the neighbor-based commands are the Law and the Prophets.* Jesus was consistent and congruent. We found this message in Jesus' Sermon on the Mount. We found this message in all of Jesus' teachings on salvation and judgment in the Gospel of Matthew. And we find this to be the message of the other Gospels as well.

So what about Paul? Did all the gospel writers portray Jesus' message one way, only to have Paul say that it was something else? Or, now that we finally have the key to the Gospels, can it be used to finally unlock the Romans code?

Puzzle #3
Romans

Chapter 17
Epiphany

The cave four Dead Sea Scrolls brought with them the missing piece necessary to unlock Paul's letter to the Romans—the Biblical book that is the cornerstone of modern Christianity. Between the cave four Dead Sea Scrolls and the early Rabbinic writings, we find that the ancients discussed two distinct kinds of *work*:

maasey hatorah[84] :	**the Works of the Law**
	(the legal jobs done for God)
maasim tovim[85] :	**good works**
	(benevolent deeds done for others)

The ancient Jewish literature associated *massim tovim* (good works) with the *gemilut chasadim* (acts of loving kindness) done to fulfill the *mitzvot bein adam lachaveiro* (commands between man and his neighbor).[86]

> Gemilut chasadim (deeds of mercy) and its nearly synonymous term *maasim tovim* (good deeds), both refer to those ethical commandments that are considered to be "acts of loving kindness" or deeds that are ethical in nature[87]

84 Dead Sea Scrolls 4QMMT and 4Q174

85 Berachot 17a, 32b (an ancient Jewish writing)

86 *Living a Jewish Life, Updated and Revised Edition: Jewish Traditions, Customs, and Values for Today's Families* by Anita Diamant, p. 61

87 *Nurturing Child and Adolescent Spirituality: Perspectives from the World's Religious Traditions* by

If the ancient Pharisees considered *maasim tovim* to fulfill the neighbor-based commands,[88] then this means that they must've used Works of the Law (*maasey hatorah*) to refer to that which was done to fulfill the commands between man and God. **In other words, the Pharisees used 'Works of the Law' as a euphemism for the *mitzvot bein adam lamakom*.** This is a historic understanding, one that explains everything.

Firstly, it fully explains Jesus' two uses of the word *work*:

> The scribes and the Pharisees sit in Moses' seat. Therefore do and keep all that they tell you. But don't do according to **their works**. For they say things and do not do them. They place heavy loads on men's shoulders, but they themselves aren't willing to lift a finger to help out.
>
> But they do all **their works** to be noticed by men. For they widen their phylacteries and lengthen the tassels of their garments.[89]

Jesus' first use of 'work' referred to 'good works' and his second use referred to some 'Works of the Law.' (The Jewish Law required the wearing of phylacteries[90] and tassels.)[91] **Jesus contrasted the two subsets of the Law using the word 'work.'** So we now have biblical confirmation that the word 'work' did indeed reflect that which is done to fulfill one subset of the Law or the other.

The Koine Greek word for 'work' used by Jesus was *ergon*. Therefore, the two Hebraisms would be:

Ergon tou nomou:	**Works of the Law**
	(the legal jobs done for God)
Ergon agathou:	**Good works**
	(benevolent deeds done for others)

Karen-Marie Yust p. 277

88 *Dictionary of Jewish Words* by Joyce Eisenberg, Ellen Scolnic, (Jewish Publication Society), p. 96. *Maasim tovim* is equivalent to *gemilut chasadim*. Therefore it is the fulfillment of the neighbor-based commandments.

89 Matthew 23:2-5

90 Deuteronomy 6:8

91 Numbers 15:38

And guess what? We find both of these Hebraisms in Paul's letter to the Romans! We find *ergon agathou* (good works) in the second chapter.

> But in accordance with your stubborn attitude, you are storing up wrath for yourself in the day when God's wrath and equitable judgment will be brought to light; who will repay each person according to his deeds: to those who eagerly seek glory, honor, and imperishability **by persisting in *ergon agathou*[92]—life in the age to come**

In the second chapter of Romans, Paul states that people inherit the kingdom because of their *ergon agathou*—because of their benevolent deeds done for others. Wow! This is the same thing Jesus taught in his quintessential teaching on judgment.

So what about the Works of the Law—the *ergon tou nomou*? What did Paul write about them?

> No one will be vindicated in God's sight through the *ergon tou nomou*

In chapter three of Romans, Paul explains that the *ergon tou nomou* (the legal jobs done for God) don't vindicate anyone.

We find that one idea flows seamlessly into another. In chapter two, Paul explains that the good works done for others (*ergon agathou*) are all that matter on judgment day. And then in chapter three, Paul explains that the Works of the Law (*ergon tou nomou*) don't matter at all.

In other words, in chapter two, Paul explains that fulfilling the neighbor-based commands is all that matters on judgment day. And in chapter three, he then explains that the commands between man and God don't matter at all. Chapter two seamlessly flows into chapter three. Together, they teach the very same thing that Jesus did.

So which denomination recognized the Works of the Law as a reference to the commands between man and God: Catholics or Protestants? The answer is: neither of them. They both missed it … big time. And their ability to understand Romans suffered as a result.

---

92 Spelled *ergou agathou* in the text. The Greek language changes the spelling of words based on how they are used within the sentence. For simplicity sake, I will use the same spelling *ergon agathou* throughout, so as to not confuse the general reader who is unfamiliar with this Greek concept.

What we now find intuitive, simple, and obvious has one major problem—it flies against fifteen hundred years of Christian tradition. The unearthing of the cave four Dead Sea Scrolls had to have sent shivers down the Church's spine. And now, we know why these scrolls were ordered to be kept secret. They completely demolish the cornerstone of fifteen hundred years of Church doctrine.

The most conclusive evidence is still to come.

For fifteen hundred years, scholars had considered the Sermon on the Mount to be a fragmented discourse. But through the use of Biblical cryptanalysis, we found that this assumption was wrong. The entire sermon was seamless from beginning to end. This seamless fluidity testifies against fifteen hundred years of Christian doctrine.

The same goes for Paul's letter to the Romans. For fifteen hundred years, scholars have considered Romans to be a fragmented discourse. But what if, through Biblical cryptanalysis, we find this assumption to be wrong? What if Biblical cryptanalysis shows us the entire letter of Romans is a seamless discourse from beginning to end? In that case, the seamless fluidity would testify against fifteen hundred years of Christian doctrine. The seamless fluidity would prove, once and for all, that Christianity has misunderstood this pivotal book for more than a millenium.

Chapter 18

99% Hebraism Free

It's really easy to see how 'good works' can refer to acts of loving kindness shown to others (i.e. "benevolent deeds"). It's also easy to see how 'Works of the Law' can refer to the jobs required by Law (i.e. the "Jobs of the Law"). Both of those phrases make intuitive sense. So the Gentiles were expected to understand these easy Hebraisms.

But they certainly couldn't be expected to intuit the complex ones. Take Jesus' introduction to his Sermon on the Mount, for example:

> Do not think I have come to **abolish** the Law or the Prophets, I did not come to **abolish** but to **fulfill**.—Jesus' introduction to his Sermon on the Mount

Gentiles couldn't be expected to know the complex Hebraisms used by Jesus. After all, Jesus used the word *katalyo,* which meant to abolish something.[93] How could they possibly know that it was a Jewish idiom which meant to **annul the Law**? And Jesus used the word *pleroo,* which meant to fulfill.[94] How could they possibly know that it was a Jewish idiom which meant to **preserve the Law**?

Paul was extremely sensitive to his Gentile readers' needs. So he converted all the complex Jewish idioms into terms that his Gentile readers could understand. I will repeat, for this is tremendously

93 BDAG, entry for *katalyo*

94 BDAG, entry for *pleroo*

important: **Paul converted all the complex Jewish idioms into terms that his Gentile readers could understand.**

Take a look at how beautifully he converted Jesus' complex Hebraism into everyday street Greek:

> Does the faith **nullify the Law**? No way! Quite the opposite, we **preserve the Law**.—Paul

Paul used the Koine word *katargeo,* which meant to nullify[95] (to annul). And Paul used *histemi,* which meant to maintain[96] (to preserve). He dutifully converted Jesus' complex Hebraic idioms into non-Hebraisms that the non-Jewish reader could understand. Aside from a handful of intuitive Hebraisms, such as 'good works' and 'Works of the Law', Paul's letter to the Romans is 99% Hebraism free.

So what does this mean when it comes to solving the puzzle? Let me ask you this: Out of all the teachings we've explored in the Gospel of Matthew, how many of them could have been understood with a knowledge of street Greek alone? Absolutely none of them could be understood based on street Greek alone. They were all written with the assumption that the reader was intimately familiar with complex Jewish idioms and ideology.

But when it comes to Romans, how many words and phrases in Paul's letter can be understood with a knowledge of street Greek alone? 99%! We're in the opposite situation, so we need to apply some opposite rules. Now all we have to do is find the best sources of Koine Greek, toss in a handful of simple Hebraisms, and we're ready to crack the code. But here's where there's a previously unwritten historical twist. The best source for Biblical Koine Greek will likely surprise you.

95 BDAG, entry for *katargeo*
96 BDAG, entry for *histemi*

Chapter 19
Bye Bye Baby Bye Bye

The Latin Vulgate was translated in the fourth century by a man named Jerome. And the Jewish Encyclopedia praises Jerome's scholarly status:

> JEROME: Church father; next to Origen, who wrote in Greek, the most learned student of the Bible among the Latin ecclesiastical writers....[97]

In fact, the encyclopedia entry is quite flattering and seeks to present Jerome in the best possible light (perhaps because he was the first Christian to attempt to study a Hebrew version of the Jewish scriptures). So how does this Jewish pro-Jerome source assess his aptitude for the Hebrew language itself?

> Jerome's knowledge of Hebrew is considerable only when compared with that of the other Church Fathers and of the general Christian public of his time. **His knowledge was really very defective.** Although he pretends to have complete command of Hebrew and proudly calls himself a "trilinguis" (being conversant with Latin, Greek, and Hebrew), he did not, in spite of all his hard work, attain to the proficiency of his simple Jewish teachers.[98]

The members of the editorial board of the Jewish Encyclopedia were, quite naturally, Hebraic experts. They had to concede that Jerome's Hebraic knowledge "was really very defective." That's a strong statement, especially when it comes from a kindly source.

---

97 *Jewish Encyclopedia*, entry for JEROME (EUSEBIUS HIERONYMUS SOPHRONIUS)
98 *Jewish Encyclopedia*, entry for JEROME (EUSEBIUS HIERONYMUS SOPHRONIUS)

This is not the only friendly source that was willing to call a spade "a spade." Consider how the noted lexicographer, Sir William Smith, a Christian, did his best to sugarcoat Jerome's "very defective" knowledge of Hebrew:

> **It would be an easy task to multiply to an almost indefinite extent the indications afforded in the writings of Jerome of his imperfect scholarship, of his unseemly haste, and of his reliance upon sources of information which were not unfrequently fallacious.** It is a more agreeable task, however, to direct attention to the very great value which his writings, especially his commentaries, possess.[99]

Sir William Smith admitted how easy it would be to find innumerable examples of Jerome's imperfect scholarship and his inability to assess the reliability of his sources. But, hey, let's just brush that aside and focus on other things, shall we? With all due respect to Sir William Smith, if we never faced this discomforting reality head on, then we would never have reclaimed Jesus' Sermon on the Mount or his essential teachings on salvation and judgment. One can only truly assess history by a willingness to admit the very severe weaknesses of some of the founders of religious doctrine—even including the Doctors of the Church.

The same goes for being willing to admit their extraordinary strengths as well. Just because Jerome's Hebraic knowledge was "really very defective", as attested by "an almost indefinite" number of examples, doesn't mean Jerome wasn't skilled in other things.

If a person has a poor grasp of Chinese, does that mean he couldn't have mastered French? If a person has a poor grasp of Russian, does that mean he couldn't have mastered Portuguese? If a person has a poor grasp of Hebraisms, does that mean he couldn't have mastered Koine Greek?

Just because a person is abysmal in one language, doesn't mean they haven't attained total mastery of another. Each language skill must be independently assessed on its own merits. And so it is with Jerome. Just because Jerome's Hebraic knowledge was "really very defective"

99 *A Dictionary of Christian Biography, Literature, Sects and Doctrines* by Sir William Smith and Henry Wace, p. 867. Sir William Smith was a noted lexicographer.

doesn't mean his Koine Greek knowledge can't be superb. So how was Jerome's Koine Greek knowledge? Is there any way to independently assess his training and exposure to Koine Greek/Latin bilingualism? Yes, there is.

Jerome lived during an interesting time, in terms of the Greek and Latin languages. He lived during the time when bilingualism was so entrenched in scholastics that students had to master their lessons in both languages. In fact, by the time Jerome was born, schools were already using *Hermeneumata*, standardized lesson books written in *both* Greek and Latin:

> The *Hermeneumata* (also called *Colloquia*), school handbooks in Greek and Latin that most likely derived from third-century Gaul[100]

These bilingual lesson books were used at all stages of education: elementary, grammar school, and the rhetorical schools of higher education as well:

> Simultaneous teaching in both languages was a common feature of Western schools. The content of the texts reveals that these books were meant for different age groups: students of elementary, grammatical, and even rhetorical schools.[101]

The papyri also attest to the extreme commonness of converting Greek to Latin (and vice versa) during Jerome's day. Forty-one bilingual (Koine Greek/Latin) glossaries were discovered among the papyri.[102] Two bilingual New Testament fragments dating to the fourth century have also been discovered.[103] And a late fifth-century Greek/Latin lexicon to some of the Pauline epistles has been found as well.[104] Jerome grew up in a bilingual population,[105] providing him with not only fluency in both Latin and Greek, but also fluency in translating from one into the other.

Yes, Jerome's Hebraic knowledge was abysmal. But his fluency

---

100 *Gymnastics of the mind: Greek education in Hellenistic and Roman Egypt* by Raffaella Cribiore p. 15

101 *Gymnastics of the mind: Greek education in Hellenistic and Roman Egypt* by Raffaella Cribiore p. 15

102 *New documents illustrating early Christianity* by G. H. R. Horsley, p. 14

103 *New documents illustrating early Christianity* by G. H. R. Horsley, p. 14

104 *New documents illustrating early Christianity* by G. H. R. Horsley, p. 14

105 *Medieval Latin: an introduction and bibliographical guide* by Frank Anthony Carl Mantello, A. G. Rigg, pp. 718-719.

in Greek and Latin was second nature. So let's keep the baby and throw out the bathwater. Let's acknowledge Jerome's inadequacy when it comes to the Hebraic book of Matthew, and simultaneously acknowledge his unique ability to enlighten us on many of the Koine Greek passages found in Romans—Paul's 99% Hebraism-free letter.

The value of Jerome's Latin Vulgate cannot be overstated. The Koine Greek language began to morph into Byzantine Greek starting in the fourth century. Jerome was tasked with unifying a set of Old Latin Bible texts originally written during the Koine period. Jerome's Latin Vulgate gives us the closest look at what the Koine Greek words meant before their meanings changed over the centuries.

For example, do you recall that Paul converted the complex Jewish idioms into the street Greek that his audience could understand? Well, the Latin Vulgate shows us something quite remarkable. It shows us how Paul discussed the two Jewish subsets of the Law in terms that his entire audience could understand:

> **If then, the uncircumcised Gentile keeps <u>the Justices of the Law</u>**, shall not this uncircumcision be counted for circumcision?[106]

> **By <u>the Works of the Law</u> no flesh shall be justified before God.**[107]

Paul referred to the neighbor-based commands as 'the Justices of the Law.' He kept the traditional 'Works of the Law' for the jobs done for God—since the phrase was pretty self-explanatory anyway. Here's where the rubber meets the road. *While the Latin Vulgate shows that Paul contrasted the two subsets of the Law, modern Bibles don't even mention the neighbor-based subset at all!* Take the NASB and NIV Bibles, for example:

> So if the uncircumcised man keeps **the requirements of the Law**, will not his uncircumcision be regarded as circumcision?—Romans 2:26 NASB

> So then, if those who are not circumcised keep **the law's requirements**, will they not be regarded as though they were circumcised?—Romans 2:26 NIV

106 Romans 2:13-14, 25-26 Latin Vulgate
107 Romans 3:20 Latin Vulgate

Where did the neighbor-based subset go? We have spent an inordinate amount of time discussing the importance of the two subset division. It's impossible to understand any conversation about first century Jewish Law without them. The Latin Vulgate shows that Paul, very early in his letter, told his converts how important it is for them to keep the Justices of the Law (the neighbor-based commands of the Law):

> Circumcision is profitable indeed, if you keep the law: but if you are a transgressor of the law, your circumcision becomes uncircumcision. **If then, the uncircumcised Gentile keeps <u>the Justices of the Law</u>**, shall not this uncircumcision be counted for circumcision?—Romans 2:26 Vulgate

Always remember, circumcision is the sign of an observer of the Law, and Gentiles are a reference to those who don't observe the Law. What Paul was saying was: If a man who keeps the Works of the Law violates the Justices of the Law, his Works of the Law count for nothing. However, if a man who doesn't keep the Works of the Law does keep the Justices of the Law, then God will judge him as if he had kept all the Works of the Law.

But when the all-important Justices of the Law are omitted from the text, it's literally impossible to know the point that Paul had written about. A negative feedback loop is thus created, for it was in chapter two that Paul contrasted the Justices of the Law, which vindicate, and the Works of the Law, which do not. The remaining fourteen chapters then build upon this foundation. However, without the reference to the Justices of the Law, erroneous meanings for all fourteen chapters must be derived, for all fourteen chapters depend on what was written before them.

So why don't modern Bibles mention the Justices of the Law? How did this happen?

When the Protestant Reformers rebelled against the Catholic Church, they decided to translate the Bible afresh directly from Greek. They wanted to break away from the Latin Vulgate. But there was only one problem: the Bible was written in Koine Greek, and none of the Reformers knew Koine Greek; in fact, they didn't know that the Koine version of Greek even existed.[108, 109] They recognized that the style of the New Testament's Greek was different from Classical Greek (the only ancient Greek they knew). But they shrugged off the differences and translated it anyway—often using meanings that were four hundred years out of date.

What happened to the Justices (*dikaiomata*) of the Law? They got rewritten. The word *dikaiomata* meant something different in Classical Greek than it did in Koine Greek. Paul's purposeful reference to the neighbor-based division of the Law was never to be seen again. For centuries to come, theologians never knew that this subset was even mentioned in the book of Romans. So they were never aware of the most fundamental aspect of first century Law around which Paul's teaching revolved. From that point forward, Paul's letter to the Romans seemed irreconcilably disconnected from Jesus' teachings in Matthew, for the key had been lost.

At this time, it is necessary to highlight a disconcerting historical fact. The Latin Vulgate's errors were primarily due to Jerome's unfamiliarity with Hebraisms. However, the non-idiomatic Koine Greek parts are quite reliable because of his Latin/Greek bilingualism. But the Protestant Reformers were unfamiliar with Hebraisms[110] and oblivious to even the prior existence of Koine Greek. So they did the unthinkable. They kept all the errors of the Latin Vulgate[111] (because of their unawareness of Hebraisms), and then they added their own errors on top[112] (because of their unawareness of Koine Greek). The loss of Paul's reference to the Justices of the Law is only one example of

108 *Basics of Biblical Greek Grammar* by William D. Mounce, chapter one

109 "The distinctive idiom of the New Testament led many scholars from the seventeen century to describe it as due to the influence of Hebrew. Other devout scholars argued that the Greek of the New Testament was the special idiom of revelation, 'the language of the Holy Ghost.' A basic solution to this critical debate was provided in the decades following 1890 when, *for the first time*, archaeology brought to light masses of papyri containing first-century non-literary Greek.... It was soon recognized that this colloquial, non-literary, *koine*, or common language, provided the basic idiom for the New Testament. For the first time biblical scholars attained a scientific understanding of the true nature of the language of the New Testament."—*New Testament and Criticism* by George Eldon Ladd, p. 87.

110 See chapter two, "Insufficient Inputs"

111 Compare the Latin Vulgate's rendering of 'evil eye' in Matthew 6 to the King James Bible as an example.

112 Compare the Latin Vulgate's translation of *dikaiomata* in Romans 2:26 to the King James Bible as one example ("the Justices of the Law" compared to "the just requirements of the Law"). The Latin Vulgate maintains the distinction of a specific subset of the Law while the King James applies an adjective to the entire Law—losing the subset distinction altogether.

many.[113] Quite remarkably, the Reformers threw out the baby and kept the bathwater. And Christianity has never been the same since.

113 Compare the Latin Vulgate's rendering of Romans 6:13 to the King James Bible as another important example. The Latin Vulgate instructs the reader to leave "injustice" to become "tools of justice for God." The King James Bible instructs the reader to leave "unrighteousness" to become "instruments of righteousness unto God." The King James Bible accords with the Classical meanings and the Latin Vulgate accords with the colloquial Koine Greek.

Chapter 20
Reset Button

In order to solve the Romans code, we must press the reset button. We need to go back in time and undo the Reformers' mistake. Whereas the Reformers kept the mistranslated Hebraisms and threw out the reliable Koine meanings, we're going to keep the reliable Koine meanings and throw out the mistranslated Hebraisms. Whereas the Reformers kept the bathwater and tossed out the baby, we're going to keep the baby and toss out the bathwater. And when we do, we find that the solution becomes a piece of cake.

So let's say goodbye to the mistranslated Hebraisms. Let's say goodbye to using Classical Greek meanings—meanings that are up to four hundred years out of date. Let's say hello to using first century culture and law to convert the Hebraisms into understandable terms, and let's say hello to Koine Greek meanings.

Our Koine Greek toolkit consists of two resources:

1. The BDAG Greek/English Lexicon Third Edition

2. The Latin Vulgate

The third edition of the BDAG lexicon was the first edition to include the Koine papyri discovered in Egypt. Now that the BDAG finally added this in (after waiting one hundred years to do so), it has tremendous value in revealing the Koine meanings of the Biblical words. But it still doesn't use the Latin Vulgate to expand the full scope of each word. So we will include this resource, which was written during a pivotal time in language history.

If the Romans text presented in the rest of this section seems foreign to you, just grab a copy of these two resources and you will discover the basis for what's written. Aside from the very few Hebraisms used by Paul,[114] all the rest of the words in Romans are Hebraism free. Now that we have a reliable way to access the actual text of Paul's letter, it's finally time to solve the Granddaddy of Biblical puzzles. It's finally time to solve the Romans code.

114 I will modernize 'good works' by rendering it as 'benevolent deeds', since it was a phrase referring to benevolent deeds done for others. I will modernize 'Works of the Law' by rendering it as 'Jobs of the Law', since it was a phrase referring to jobs done for God (a connotation that Paul references in his employment metaphor in Romans chapter four). This modernization will help bypass centuries of indoctrinated emotional attachment to the meaning of the phrases 'good works' and 'Works of the Law' by avoiding the use of these terms altogether.

Chapter 21
Methodology

Our methodology for breaking the Romans code is quite straightforward. We shall crack the code by examining the letter from three perspectives (in a very specific order):

- How does the letter connect to Jesus' essential teachings?
- What issues regarding Jesus' teachings is the letter seeking to address?
- How does Paul address each issue?

Chapter 22
Pauly Wants a Cracker

I'm going to propose something that's probably going to sound outrageous: Orthodox Christianity never developed a seamless reconciliation of Paul's letter to the Romans with Jesus' teachings in Matthew because they misunderstood Jesus himself. And the proof is in the pudding. From the moment we restore Jesus' original teachings, we find that Paul not only agreed with Jesus, he actually parroted him:

> Don't think that I have come to put an end to the Law. I have not come to abolish but to preserve it down to the tiniest commandment.[115]—Jesus
>
> Does the faith nullify the Law? No way! Quite the opposite, we preserve the Law.[116]—Paul

Jesus contrasted nullifying and preserving (via Jewish idioms) and Paul parrots Jesus' teaching (via Koine Greek). Once we understand what Jesus taught, we don't even need to try to reconcile Paul's teaching, for Paul mimicked the same idea. They're already the same.

> If you want to enter into that life, keep the commandments."
>
> The man said to him, "Which kind?"
>
> And Jesus said, "**Don't murder, don't be unfaithful, don't steal,** don't lie, honor your father and mother—**love your neighbor as yourself.**"[117]—Jesus

115 Matthew 5:17

116 Romans 3:31

117 Matthew 19:16-19

> He who loves others has fulfilled the Law. For **'don't be unfaithful,' 'don't murder,' 'don't steal,'** 'don't covet,' and if there be any other commandment it is recapitulated in this one statement, in the saying, "**Love your neighbor as yourself.**"[118]—Paul

As you may recall, the Ten Commandments were divided into two subsets: the first four commandments were based on loving God and the remaining six were based on the love of neighbor. Jesus cited five of the six commands based on the love of neighbor. Then he clarified that he was referring to all the commandments recapitulated by "love your neighbor as yourself." Paul parroted not only Jesus' teaching, but even his strategy as well. Paul cited four out of the six commands based on the love of neighbor. Then he clarified that he was referring to all commandments recapitulated by "love your neighbor as yourself."

Once again, we see how easy it is to reconcile Paul with Jesus … now that we know what Jesus was saying in the first place.

Let's keep going.

> In everything treat others the same way you want to be treated for this is the Law[119]—Jesus

In first century Jewish speak, Jesus was saying:

> Only the neighbor-based commands are the Law; the Jobs of the Law are not.—Jesus

Jesus assured his audience that the faith he was promoting contained a Law, just not one of jobs. Paul conveyed the exact same thing to his Roman converts:

> Where then is boasting? It is excluded. Through which kind of Law? The one of jobs? By no means! Rather, by faith's Law.[120]

Once again, Pauly wants a cracker. The Christian faith has a law. But the Christian faith's law doesn't contain any of the jobs done for God.

118 Romans 13:8-10

119 Matthew 7:12

120 Romans 3:20

Jesus said that humanity will be divided into two groups based solely on their altruism. Those who treated others benevolently will inherit life. And the rest (the selfish and unjust) will receive rage and wrath. Would you be surprised to know that Paul taught the very same thing?

> But in accordance with your stubborn attitude you are storing up wrath for yourself in the day when God's wrath and equitable judgment will be brought to light; who will repay each person according to his deeds: To those who eagerly seek glory, honor, and imperishability through persisting in benevolent deeds[121] —life in the age to come; to those who are selfish, resisting the truth (in being yielded to injustice)—rage and wrath.[122]

Paul parroted Jesus once again, for Paul also taught that humanity will be divided into two groups based solely on the benevolence of their deeds.

Let's checkout one more teaching of Jesus' dutifully repeated by Paul:

> I tell you the truth, unless you treat people better than the religious leaders you cannot enter the kingdom of God[123]—Jesus

> Witness the kindness and severity of God! To those who fell—severity; yet to you—kindness (if you persist in kindness otherwise you also will be cut off).[124]—Paul

Jesus warned his followers that if they didn't treat others kindly, then they would be cut off from the kingdom of heaven. Paul warned his followers about the very same thing.

So you see, once we know what Jesus taught, it's really not that hard to reconcile Paul with him, because they both taught the very same thing:

- The Law remains intact.
- But only the neighbor-based commands are the Law.

121 Paul used the Koine Greek equivalent of the Hebrew idiom *maasim tovin* (lit. good works, idiom for: benevolent deeds done for others).

122 Romans 2:5-8

123 Matthew 5:20 (see chapter three, "Biblical Code Breaking")

124 Romans 11:12

- And the Jobs done for God aren't the Law.
- Each person will be judged based solely on the benevolence of their deeds.
- So if Christians don't treat others kindly, they are going to be cut off.

But the reconciliation doesn't come without its casualties. For even during this stage of the investigation, we can't help running into an explosive bombshell.

Chapter 23
Bombshell

Philo Judaeus, a contemporary of Jesus, belonged to a prominent Alexandrian Jewish family. His forefathers were granted Roman citizenship. Philo's education included Hellenistic and Roman culture in addition to his studies in the Jewish traditions. This mix of cultures is quite fortunate. Through his writings, we get to see how a first century Jew explained Jewish customs to the non-Jewish population. One particular explanation resolves an ancient and explosive mystery.

Consider Philo's explanation of the two divisions of the Jewish Law:

> And there are, as we may say, two most especially important heads of all the innumerable particular lessons and doctrines; the regulating of one's conduct towards God by the rules of piety and holiness, and of one's conduct towards men by the rules of humanity and justice; each of which is subdivided into a great number of subordinate ideas, all praiseworthy.[125]

Alright, so what's so incredible about that? We've already seen numerous sources showing that the Jews divided the Law into two subsets: commands between man and God, and commandments between man and his neighbor. But what we didn't have before was the first century nature of the division. Philo's description of the nature of the division explains some of the most explosive Biblical texts … including the writings of Paul

125 *The Special Laws* 2.63 by Philo Judaeus

Bear with me, because what I'm about to say may sound impossible. Yet, I'll prove it to be so by the end of the chapter. Let's step back into the first century Jewish mindset. As a first century Jew, we know that man keeps himself pure as a tribute to God. All the holiness commands (all the purity commands) are commands between man and God. Now, this Jesus of Nazareth gets up on the Mount of Olives, and promises to give an interpretation of scripture that encompasses every commandment down to the smallest one. Yet, the sermon focuses exclusively on neighbor-based commands and what God can do for you. And then, in keeping with the rest of the sermon, Jesus has the audacity to state: Only the neighbor-based commands are the Law; the other commandments are not—including the sexual purity commands.

The crowd's reaction would likely have been the same as you may be having right now. And their reasoning would probably be similar: *Everyone knows God won't let the sexually impure into the kingdom ... I mean, everyone knows that.*

Let's consider Jesus' quintessential teaching on judgment, for the definition of Law and the judgment day standard are inseparable. In his quintessential teaching on judgment, Jesus said that humanity will be divided into two groups based solely on the benevolence of their deeds. What happens to the sexually impure person who makes the humanitarian needs of others equal to his own? Both Jesus' Law and his judgment teaching allow this person, who abused his body, to still inherit life in the kingdom. To say otherwise would be to collapse the entire structure of Jesus' Sermon on the Mount. To say otherwise would be to collapse the entire premise of Jesus' quintessential teaching on judgment. To say otherwise would be to deny that all God wants is loving kindness for the forgiveness of sins (as Hosea prophesied and Jesus concurred). What in the world does the ultra-conservative Paul have to say about this? The answer's going to surprise you.

As we discussed in the previous chapter, Paul's letter to the Romans parroted Jesus' teaching on judgment:

> But in accordance with your stubborn attitude you are storing up wrath for yourself in the day when God's wrath and equitable judgment will be

> brought to light; who will repay each person according to his deeds: To those who eagerly seek glory, honor, and imperishability through persisting in benevolent deeds[126] —life in the age to come; to those who are selfish, resisting the truth (in being yielded to injustice[127])—rage and wrath.[128]

In this passage, Paul says that humanity will be split into two groups with the benevolent on one side and the selfish/unjust on the other. Okay, so far sounds like Jesus. But Paul's lead-in is much more specific. Here's the passage that comes right before the one above:

> And as they tried not to prove the things of God via examination, **God handed them over to a worthless mind to do unallowable things**: full of every injustice, licentious wantonness, worthlessness, greed, and maliciousness; full of envy,[129] discord, deceit, meanspiritedness, and rumors; they speak bad of others and abhor the existence of God; they insult, proudly brag, invent ways to inflict physical pain and disobey their parents; they are untrustworthy and they break their contracts.
>
> They are heartless, hostile and unmerciful. And while they recognize **God's requirement of justice (that those who spend their time this way deserve death)** they not only spend their time this way, but they also give their consent to others who spend their time this way as well.[130]

First, it's important to notice that Paul wrote that those who do the *unallowable* things deserve spiritual death. Second, it's important to notice that all the unallowable things worthy of death are examples of self-centeredness or injustice.

---

126 Hebraism based on the Hebrew idiom *maasim tovin* (idiom for benevolent deeds done for others).

127 Koine Greek: *adikia*. See Latin Vulgate.

128 Romans 2:5-8

129 Some manuscripts include 'murder', which is likely a copyist error. The Greek word for 'murder' is spelled the same as the Greek word for 'envy', minus one letter. Very often, in lists where 'murder' follows 'envy' (or vice versa) a copyist error has occurred. Notice also how 'murder' does not belong in a list of things which people 'are full of'.

130 Romans 1:26-32

Paul's List of Unallowable Things

Selfish, Self-centered Living	Yielded to Injustice
Full of licentious wantonness—living only for sexual pleasure	Full of every inequity—treating others inequitably in every way
Full of worthlessness—doing nothing to help others	Full of maliciousness
Full of greed	Sowing Discord
Full of envy	Deceitful
Abhor the existence of God—wanting to do only whatever they please. They hate the idea of a God who demands they treat others kindly. (See Romans 3:11-18)	Mean-spirited
Proud	Spread Rumors
Braggarts	Speak badly of others
Disobey their parents	Insulting
Heartless	Inventing ways to physically harm others
Unmerciful	Breaking their word and their contracts
	Hostile

So there's a flow here. First, Paul gives an example of the unallowable things that deserve spiritual death—all the examples being selfish and unjust acts. Then he declares that the selfish and unjust will suffer the wrath of God.

But wait! There's more! Now, let's take a look at the passage that came before the unallowable things that deserve spiritual death:

> On account of this, **God handed them over to <u>dishonorable</u> passions.** For both their females quit instinctual function for one contrary to instinct. And in the same way, indeed, the males quit the instinctual use of the female burning away in their lust for one another—males with males—resulting in disgraceful acts, **and they <u>received in themselves the full penalty</u> necessary for their error.**

And here's the bombshell. Paul writes about the *dishonorable* (sexual) passions in which people *receive in their bodies* the full penalty for those actions. That's right. Paul separated the dishonorable sins that harm the body from the unallowable sins that cost the soul.[131] He then doubled down on the separation by specifying that only the selfish, unjust, unallowable things matter on judgment day. What Jesus implied, Paul made explicit.

But why did Paul bother drawing a hard line between the consequences of sexual promiscuity and the consequences of licentious wantonness? He had to! If Paul declared sexuality as an unallowable thing deserving spiritual death, then he'd be rejecting Jesus' teaching that only the neighbor-based commands are the Law. Paul wasn't going to reject Jesus' teaching. Paul wasn't going to reject Jesus. And he didn't.

131 Paul's separation of sexual sins which harm the body vs. ethical sins which harm the soul is found throughout his other writings. See *The Jesus Secret* by Michael Wood, chapter 13, "The Non-Mortal Sins," for detailed documentation of this.

Chapter 24
The Issues

So we're done with the first step of our code-breaking process. We've discovered the places where Paul's letter connects with Jesus' essential teachings:

Teaching	Paul	Jesus
The Law remains intact	Romans 3:31	Matthew 5:17
But only the neighbor based commands are the Law.	Romans 13:8-10	Matthew 19:16-19
The jobs done for God aren't the Law.	Romans 3:20	Matthew 7:12
Each person will be judged based solely on the benevolence of their deeds.	Romans 2:5-8	Matthew 25:31-46
So if Christians don't treat others kindly, they are going to be cut off.	Romans 11:12	Matthew 5:20

Paul's doctrines are based on the same premise which encompasses all of Jesus' teachings on salvation and judgment in the Gospel of Matthew: *Jesus did not come to abolish the Law and the*

Prophets because only the neighbor-based commands are the Law and the Prophets. In fact, we found that Paul embraced Jesus' premise so fully, that he even applied it to his discussions on sexuality as well.

Now that we've identified how Paul's letter reiterates Jesus' essential teaching, it's time to move to the next phase of breaking the Romans code. We need to explore the issues that Paul's Roman converts were having with Jesus' teaching.

So let's find out.

> Therefore, you have no excuse, all of you who are judging others. For that in which you judge others you condemn yourself because you do the very same things yourself.[132]

The first group that Paul addresses in his letter is the Hypocrites. These folks were judging others for violating the neighbor-based commands, while they themselves were breaking the very same neighbor-based commands. Paul deals with these folks in Romans 1:17-2:16.

Let's take a look at who Paul addresses next.

> Pay attention! You who are named a Jew and take comfort in the Law and boast in God.[133]

The next group that Paul addresses is the Judaizers. The Judaizers believed that the Jobs of the Law[134] (the commandments between man and God) were the source of their vindication. Therefore, they considered the benevolent deeds done for others[135] (the commandments between man and neighbor) to be optional, if not unnecessary. Paul deals with these folks in Romans 2:17-5:21.

Let's take a look at who Paul addresses next.

> What then, shall we 'continue in sin that the favor might super-proliferate?'[136]

132 Romans 2:1

133 Romans 2:17

134 Jobs of the Law: *maasey hatorah* (Hebrew), *ergon tou nomou* (Koine Greek).

135 Benevolent deeds done for others: *maasim tovin* (Hebrew), *ergon agathou* (Koine Greek)

136 Romans 6:1

The next group that Paul addresses is the Mental. The Mental believed they would be saved from God's wrath because of what they mentally believed, not because of their actions. They misunderstood the nature of the favor of Christ. They didn't understand that Christ's favor was to free them from the Jobs of the Law. They didn't understand Jesus' teaching that God would save people simply as a favor for truly loving others the same as themselves. Because they misunderstood the nature of the favor, they actually thought God's 'favor' would be increased by their mistreatment of their neighbors! Paul deals with these folks in Romans 6:1-8:27.

Let's take a look at who Paul addresses next.

> What Israel searched for, this it did not obtain; rather those who were selected obtained it, and the rest who were not selected were made blind.... But if some of the branches were cut off, and you a wild olive tree were grafted in to share in the root and of the sap of the olive tree, don't gloat over the branches! You who are gloating don't support the root.[137]

The final group that Paul deals with is the Predestined Proud. These folks were gloating over the idea that natural-born Jews were predestined to be cut off in order for them to be grafted in. Paul deals with the conceited gloating of the Predestined Proud in Romans 8:28-11:36.

And that's it! That's the very simple structure of Paul's letter to the Romans:

Greetings	(1:1-1:16)
The Hypocrites	(1:17-2:16)
The Judaizers	(2:17-5:21)
The Mental	(6:1-8:27)
The Predestined Proud	(8:28-11:36)
Ending	(12:1-16:26)

137 Romans 11:7, 17-18

So now that we've identified the issues that Paul's letter was addressing, it's time to take a look at how he dealt with each of them.

Chapter 25
The Hypocrites

The first group that Paul addresses in his letter is the Hypocrites:

> Therefore, you have no excuse, all of you who are judging others. For that in which you judge others you condemn yourself because you do the very same things yourself.[138]

So let's take a look at what exactly the Hypocrites were doing:

138 Romans 2:1

IMPORTANT NOTE

For faster reading you can skip over all the Romans passages and simply read the commentary that comes after them. Should you have any questions regarding the commentary, you can refer to the passage above it.

Romans 2:3-11

But do you think this (you who judge others while you also doing these things yourself) that you shall escape the judgment of God? Or do you disdain the wealth of his kindness, tolerance, and leniency; not knowing that God's kindness leads you to changing your mentality?

But in accordance with your stubborn attitude, you are storing up wrath for yourself in the day when God's wrath and equitable judgment will be brought to light; who will repay each person according to his deeds: to those who eagerly seek glory, honor, and imperishability by persisting in benevolent deeds—life in the age to come; to those who are selfish, resisting the truth (in being yielded to injustice)—rage and wrath.

Affliction and distress will be upon every soul of man who does malicious things, both the Jew (first) and the Gentile. But glory, honor, and peace will be to all engaged in benevolent actions, both to the Jew (first) and to the Gentile. For there is no partiality with God.

The Hypocrites appear to believe that just because they are Christians, they won't be judged according to the way they treat their fellow man. So Paul warns them that absolutely everyone, themselves included, will be judged according to their benevolence. No one, including themselves, will escape the equitable judgment of God. Those who do benevolent deeds will inherit life in the age to come, while the selfish and malicious will receive rage and wrath.

There could be no clearer connection to Jesus' Sermon on the Mount. The benevolent are those who follow the Golden Rule. There are two types of people who violate it: those who selfishly ignore the needs of others and those who treat others maliciously. According to Paul, one day, God will judge everyone (Christian and non-Christian alike) according to their deeds—according to the Golden Rule.

Summary

The Hypocrites: Roman Christians who were condemning others for breaking neighbor-based commands while they themselves were doing the very same things.

The Smack Down: Paul assures the Hypocrites that they will be judged in the very same way as the rest of the world—according to the benevolence of their deeds. And if they continue in their selfish and malicious ways, they will certainly suffer God's wrath.

Chapter 26
The Judaizers

The next group that Paul dealt with in his letter was the Judaizers:

> Pay attention! You who are named a Jew and take comfort in the Law and boast in God.[139]

The Judaizers took comfort in keeping all the commandments between man and God. They believed their adherence to the Works of the Law—the Jobs of the Law—vindicated them in God's sight.

So what was so wrong with them keeping the Jobs of the Law? Why was Paul so upset with them anyway?

> **Romans 2:21-24**
>
> You then, you who teach others, do you not teach yourself? You who tell others not to steal, you steal! You who say to not commit adultery, you commit adultery! And you who hate idols, you forcibly rob items from temples! You who boast in the Law, by your violation of the Law you disrespect God. Just as it has been written, "The name of God is maligned among the nations because of you."

The problem wasn't with the Jobs of the Law, per se. The problem was that these folks were stealing, committing adultery, and raiding temples—they were keeping the Jobs of the Law while mistreating their fellow man at the same time. Even though these folks

139 Romans 2:17

were breaking the neighbor-based commands, they were convinced of their vindication because of their faithfulness to the Jobs of the Law.

So Paul warned them that their violation of the neighbor-based commands was disrespectful to God. The name of God was being maligned far and wide because of them. Then he continued to put them in their place by delivering a shocking rebuke:

> **Romans 2:25-27**
>
> For indeed circumcision has benefit if you are doing things according to the Law, but if you are a violator of the Law then your circumcision becomes uncircumcision. And **if then the uncircumcised Gentile fulfills the Justices of the Law, will not his uncircumcision be counted as circumcision? And the uncircumcised Gentile (who is instinctively fulfilling the Law) will judge you** who are from the letter of the law and circumcision who violate the Law.

Paul tells the Judaizers that the Jobs of the Law, such as circumcision, have value *only if they are keeping the Justices of the Law (Paul's Koine Greek reference to the neighbor-based commands).* And then, he shames them. He tells them that unbelieving Gentiles who instinctively fulfill the neighbor-based commands will be the judges of the Christian Jews who do not!

It's important to note that Paul mentions unbelieving Gentiles who instinctively keep the neighbor-based commands three times in his letter:

> It's not the listeners of the Law who are vindicated before God, rather the doers of the Law will be vindicated). For example, **when Gentiles who don't have the Law do the things of the Law, they are a Law unto themselves; in that they show the purpose of the Law written on their hearts;**[140]
>
> * * *
>
> For indeed circumcision has benefit if you are doing things according to the Law, but if you are a violator of the Law then your circumcision becomes uncircumcision. And if then the uncircumcised Gentile fulfills the Justices of the Law, will not his uncircumcision be counted as circumcision? And **the uncircumcised Gentile (who is instinctively fulfilling the Law) will**

140 Romans 2:13-15

judge you who are from the letter of the law and circumcision who violate the Law.[141]

* * *

For the Law produces wrath; for **even where there is no law there are those who don't violate it.**[142]

Paul continually marveled at how the Jobs of the Law caused the Jewish nation to ignore the purpose of the Law—the benevolent treatment of their fellowman. It seems that he was stunned to find, during his journey among the Gentiles, that many of them were keeping the purpose of the Law instinctively by nature. He struggled to understand why the Law made it so hard for his fellow Jews to do the same.

Now Paul had his hands full. Over the millennia, the Jewish nation had developed a tight-knit theology that made it hard for him to change their minds. He had a number of Jewish theological issues to deal with:

- The Jews believed the Jobs of the Law gave them an advantage over non-Jews.
- The Jews heralded Abraham as an example of vindication through devoted deeds done for God. Therefore, they heralded Abraham as an example of why devotion to the Jobs of the Law is necessary.
- The Jews believed each person has an individual responsibility to perform the Jobs of the Law in order to mend man's broken relationship with God.

So let's see how Paul dealt with each of these Jewish theological issues.

141 Romans 2:25-27
142 Romans 4:15

Romans 3:9-23

What then, don't us Jews have an advantage over others? Absolutely not. For as we've shown before, **both Jews and Greeks are all under sin.** Just as it has been written, "There's no one equitable, not even one. No one gets it. No one's seeking after God. Everyone together avoids him, becoming useless. **There isn't anyone showing loving kindness, not even one. Their throat is an open tomb. They deceive with their tongues. The poison of snakes is under their lips; whose mouth is filled with curses and bitterness. Their feet are eager to shed blood. Destruction and misery lay in their paths. The way of peace they have never known.** There is no reverence of God before their eyes." And we know that as much as the Law says, it says to those who are in the Law; that every mouth should be silenced and the whole world be made accountable to God.

This is why no one will be vindicated by the Jobs of the Law: because through the Law comes consciousness of sin. And now **a justice of God without observance of the Law** has manifested, which is attested by the Law and the Prophets; the justice of the faith of Jesus the Messianic King unto all and on all who entrust themselves to it without distinction **for all have missed the mark and come short of the glory of God.**

The first theological issue that Paul deals with is 'the presumed Jewish advantage.' Paul uses the Jewish scriptures in a very clever way. He demonstrates to the Jews that their own scriptures show that there was a time when none of the Jews or Gentiles was kind and compassionate. Rather, everyone was deceitful, bitter, murderous, destructive, hurtful and chaotic.

Paul explains that this is why the Jews can never be vindicated by the Jobs of the Law. Through the Law's neighbor-based commands came a consciousness of sin,[143] and yet, the Jewish race violated them anyway. For this reason, the Jobs of the Law will not vindicate anyone. They have mistreated their fellowman so much that the Jobs of the Law can't possibly make up for their shortcomings.

And now, Jesus has introduced a faith that includes *a justice*

143 In Romans 13:9, Paul lists "Do not covet" as a command recapitulated in the statement, "Love you neighbor as yourself." In other words, he classified it as a neighbor-based command. He uses this neighbor-based command in Romans chapter seven to illustrate the concept of 'the neighbor-based commands bringing an awareness (consciousness) of sin.'

apart from the Jobs of the Law as attested by the Law and the Prophets: "In everything, therefore, treat others the same way you want to be treated for this is the Law and the Prophets."[144] Only those who entrust themselves to it will be justified, for both Jews and Gentiles have fallen short of the glory of God through their unkind treatment of others. Therefore everyone, Jews and Gentiles alike, must follow the neighbor-based justice of Jesus' faith if they want to be vindicated before God.

Let's take a look at the next Jewish theological issue that Paul had to deal with:

REMINDER

For faster reading you can skip over all the Romans passages and simply read the commentary that comes after them. Should you have any questions regarding the commentary, you can refer to the passage above it.

Romans 3:24-5:5

We are freely vindicated through his favor, the salvation which is in Jesus the Messianic King; whom God set forth as an appeasement in his blood through the faith; for a demonstration of his justice through **the passing over of sins previously committed**, for a demonstration of his justice in the present time in God's clemency; for his being one of justice and his vindicating him who belongs to Jesus' faith.

Where then is boasting? It has been excluded. **Through what kind of Law? A Law of jobs? No, but through faith's Law. For we consider a man to be vindicated by faith independent of the Jobs of the Law.** Or is God only of the Jews? But is he not also of the nations? Yes, also of the nations. Since indeed there is one God who shall vindicate the circumcised through faith and vindicate the uncircumcised through the faith. **Does the faith nullify the Law? No way! Quite the opposite, we preserve the Law.**

What then shall we say Abraham our father has found according to circumcision of the flesh? For if Abraham was vindicated because of jobs he has a right to boast. But not toward God. For what does the scripture say? "But Abraham trusted God and it was credited to him as vindication.

144 Jesus in Matthew 7:12

And to the one who is employed, the wage is not credited as a favor, but as an obligation. But to the one who is not employed, but trusts the one who vindicates the impious, his trust is credited as vindication. Just as also David says about the blessing of the man whom God vindicates independent of doing any jobs. "Blessed are those who were forgiven their violations of the Law and whom the sins were covered over. Blessed is the man in whom the Lord will not credit the sin." Then is this blessing upon the circumcised or also upon the uncircumcised?

For we say that **the trust was credited to Abraham as vindication. How then was it credited? Was it credited while he was circumcised or uncircumcised? It wasn't credited while he was circumcised, but while he was uncircumcised.** And he received the sign of circumcision as a seal of the vindication of the trust of those who are uncircumcised; in order that he might be a father of everyone who trusts through uncircumcision so the vindication might be credited to them also. And he is the father of circumcision not only to those who are physically circumcised, but also to the ones who walk to the footsteps of the faith; the ones in the uncircumcision of our father Abraham.

The promise wasn't made to Abraham or to his descendents through observance of the Law. But in order for him to be heir of the world it was through the vindication of trust. **For if the ones observing the Law are heirs, then the faith has no effect, and the promise is nullified. For the Law produces wrath; for even where there is no law there are those who don't violate it.** On account of this it is of trust, that according to the favor, for the promise to be firm to all descendents; not only to those who are of the Law, but also those who are of the trust of Abraham, who is the father of us all. Just as it was written, "I have made you father of many nations." In front of which he trusted God, the one restoring the dead to life, and calling the ones not existing as existing; who, against hope in hope did trust, in order for him to become a father of many nations; according to that which was said, "So shall your descendents be."

And not being weak in trust, he didn't consider his own body which was already deadened (as he was approximately one hundred years old), nor did he consider the deadness of Sarah's womb. And at that promise of God he did not judge the situation in distrust, but was strengthened in his trust, giving praise to God, fully convinced that God is able to do that which he promised. Therefore also it was credited to him as vindication. But it was not for his benefit only that it was credited, but also for our benefit, to the ones who it will be credited in the future , to those trusting the one who raised Jesus our master from dead; who was handed over on account of our wrongdoing, and was raised on account of our vindication.

> Being vindicated by trust, we have peace towards God through our master Jesus the Messianic King; through whom we also have access to the faith in this favor in which we stand firm and pride ourselves upon in hope of the glory of God. And not only that, be we also pride ourselves in our sufferings, knowing that suffering creates perseverance, perseverance creates proven character, proven character creates hope, and the hope does not disappoint because the love of God has been poured out in our hearts through the holy spirit that has been given to us.

This very long passage has been butchered by the modern convention of using chapters, verses, and subheadings. This is one continuous passage from start to finish. When the flow gets interrupted, a lot of crazy ideas can be misconstrued from it.

The first thing that Paul introduces is Jesus' appeasement of sins that have been *previously* committed. Somehow, this passage gets twisted and contorted to make Abraham an example of the appeasement of all sins—past, present, and future. Most people are unaware that Paul introduces this passage with a discussion on how *previously* committed sins are forgiven.

Second, after introducing the concept of appeasement for previously committed sins, Paul then posits the question: Does the forgiveness of previously committed sins abolish the Law? He firmly declares that it's actually the opposite: It validates the Law. The Christian faith preserves the Law.

Third, Paul then explains how the appeasement and fulfillment of the Law work together. Paul explains that the Christian faith has a different *kind of Law* than the one the Judaizers rely upon. The Judaizers' Law is based on jobs while the Christian Law is not. This is consistent with Paul's earlier statement that the Christian Law is composed solely of the Justices of the Law (the neighbor based commandments).[145]

Fourth, to show that the Jobs of the Law are not necessary for previously committed sins to be forgiven, Paul then uses Abraham as a scriptural example. Abraham was chosen for a very specific reason. The first century Jewish nation cherished Abraham's vindication before

145 In Romans 2:13-15, 26 Paul wrote that those who keep the *dikaiomata tou nomou* (the Justices of the Law) are the doers of the Law who are vindicated before God. This is the subset of commandments that remain intact within the Christian faith.

God via his faithful deeds.[146, 147, 148] In fact, James (the brother of Jesus) himself heralded Abraham's vindication through faithfulness.

> Wasn't Abraham our father vindicated by deeds when he offered up Isaac his son on the altar?[149]

So Paul reminded his Jewish audience of something they probably hadn't considered before: Abraham was *initially* vindicated the moment he trusted God. And more than that, Abraham's *initial* vindication came before circumcision (and any of the other Jobs of the Law) ever existed. Thus, Abraham is a scriptural example of why the Jobs of the Law are not necessary for the forgiveness of previously committed sins.

Did Paul contradict James' statement that Abraham's ongoing vindication was based on his deeds? Of course not! Paul had already stated that Christians will be judged by the benevolence of their deeds. So now, Paul is simply pointing out that the passing over of Abraham's previously committed sins occurred the moment he trusted God. And James showed that Abraham's vindication continued from that point forward based on his deeds, which is fully consistent with what Paul had already told the Hypocrites.

Let's take a look at the next Jewish theological issue that Paul had to deal with.

146 "And when Abraham was tested he was found faithful. Therefore the Lord assured him with an oath that he would be blessed through his posterity." Sirach 44:20

147 "Was not Abraham found faithful when he was tested, and it was reckoned to him as justice?" 1 Maccabees 2:52

148 "Abraham, then, filled with zeal for piety, the highest and greatest of virtues, was eager to follow God and to be obedient to his commands." *On Abraham* by Philo Judaeus (a first century contemporary of Paul), paragraph 60.

149 James 2:21

Romans 5:6-21

For while we were still feeble, at the proper time the Messiah King died for the impious. For rarely will a person die even for an equitable man, though maybe for such a man someone might be willing to die. But God shows his own love for us in that, while we were still sinners, the Messianic King died for us. Much more then, having been vindicated in his blood, we will be saved by him from the wrath. For if being enemies we were reconciled to God through the death of his son, much more having been reconciled will we be saved in his life. And not only that, but **we also pride ourselves in God through our master Jesus the Messianic King, through whom we have now obtained the reconciliation.**

On account of this, just as through one man sin entered the world (and through sin entered death which therefore went through to all men because all men sinned). Because prior to the Law, sin was in the world but sin wasn't charged, given there wasn't a Law. But death reigned from Adam until Moses; reigning even upon those who didn't sin in the likeness of Adam's violation, who is an archetype of the one about to come. **But shouldn't the favor also be in the same manner as the transgression? For if the many died because of one man's transgression, to many more the favor of God (and the gift by favor) proliferate to the many because of one man—Jesus the Messianic King.** And the gift is not like one act of sin. For indeed the judgment of the one act brought condemnation, yet the favor brings out of many transgressions, vindication.

For if in the transgression of the one act death reigned via the one act, how more the ones receiving the abundance of favor and the gift of vindication shall reign in life through the one act of Jesus the Messianic King. Therefore, then, as through one transgression came condemnation to all men, so also through one equitable deed came vindication to life to all men. For just as by the disobedience of the one man many were established as sinners, so also by the obedience of one man many shall be vindicated. But Law entered in secretly that transgression should super-proliferate. But where sin was superabundant the favor super-proliferated, that just as sin reigned in death, so also the favor should reign through vindication to the life of the age to come through Jesus the Messianic King our master.

This passage is very easy to understand the moment we consider the Jewish theological issue that Paul was addressing: Each person has the individual responsibility to perform the Jobs of the Law in order to mend his broken relationship with God. Paul undercuts this theology by once again appealing to the Jewish scriptures. He reminds the Jews that their own scriptures say that humanity's relationship was broken because of one man—Adam. And so, Paul then posits: If humanity's relationship to God can be broken because of only one being, couldn't it also be restored by the act of one being? Paul uses this logic, drawn from scripture, to affirm why the Jobs of the Law are not necessary to repair our broken relationship to God. For through the one act of Jesus the Messianic King, humanity has already been reconciled to God. It's as if all humanity has perfectly kept the Jobs of the Law. Now, as we shall see, Paul quickly clarifies that humanity's one remaining obligation is to the altruistic treatment of his fellowman.

Summary

The Judaizers: These were Jewish folks who believed they were vindicated before God by performing the Jobs of the Law—even though they were stealing, committing adultery, and destroying other's temples.

The Smack Down: No flesh, including theirs, will be vindicated by the Jobs of the Law.

Counter Points: Jews have no advantage over non-Jews, because through the Law's neighbor-based commands, came an awareness of sin and the Jewish nation massively sinned anyway.

Abraham is a scriptural example of someone whose previously committed sins were passed over without the Jobs of the Law.

Adam shows that if humanity's relationship to God can be broken through the act of one, then humanity's relationship to God can be restored through the act of one.

Chapter 27
The Mental

Now we come to another issue, one that somehow has been resurrected from the dead in the sixteenth century: The Mental. The Mental were Roman Gentiles who misunderstood Paul's Jewish examples. They didn't understand the distinction between different types of Laws. They didn't understand Paul's teachings about faithful Abraham. And so on and so on.

Because they didn't understand the Jewish discussions, they came up with a terrible misinterpretation. They believed that they had no obligation to any part of the Law, including the neighbor-based commands. They believed that all sins—past, present, and future—were covered over the moment they trusted in Christ. They believed that Christ's favor was to forgive them of all their sins—past, present, and future—regardless of what they do. And therefore, they concluded that they could increase the size of the favor by sinning more and more and more:

> What then, shall we 'continue in sin that the favor might super-proliferate?'[150]

So did Paul believe that it was even possible for a Christian to "continue in sin that the favor might super-proliferate?"

150 Romans 6:1

Romans 6:1-23

What then, shall we 'continue in sin that the favor might super-proliferate?' No way! We died to sin. How shall we still live in it? Or don't you know that all who were baptized unto Messianic King Jesus were baptized into his death? We were buried together with him through baptism into death; so that just as Messianic King rose from the dead by the majesty of the father, so also we should be walking in a brand new life. For if we've been planted together in the likeness of his death, so also of the likeness of his resurrection we shall be. Knowing this, that our old self was crucified along with him, that the body of sin should be rendered powerless, that we are no longer sin's slaves. **For the one who dies has been vindicated from sin.** And if we died along with the Messianic King, we believe we will also live along with him. Knowing that the Messianic King, having been raised from the dead, no longer dies; death no longer has mastery over him, because the death he died, he died to sin once for all; and the life he lives, he lives to God. So also you consider yourselves dead to sin and alive to God, in Jesus the Messianic King our master.

Therefore don't let sin rule in your mortal body, obeying it in what it wants. Nor offer the members of your body to as tools of injustice. But offer yourselves to God as one living out of the dead, and your members to God as tools of justice. For sin shall not be your master, because you are not subservient to the Law, but subservient to the favor.

What then, 'shall we sin since we are not subservient to the Law but subservient to the favor?' No way! **Don't you know that to whomever you offer yourselves as obedient slaves, you are slaves of the one you are obeying: either sin unto death, or obedience unto vindication. But thanks be to God, for though you once were slaves to sin, you obeyed from the heart the construct of the teaching to which you were entrusted. And having been emancipated from sin, you became slaves to justice.**

I am speaking in human terms on account of the feebleness of your flesh, for as you offered your members subservient to unethical behavior and to lawlessness (unto lawlessness), so now render your members subservient to justice unto total dedication. For when you were sin's slaves, you were not obliged to do justice. What result did you have from the things in which you are now ashamed? For the end result of those things is death.

But now, having been emancipated from the sin, and having become God's slaves, you have your result unto total dedication, which results in life in the age to come. For the cost of sin is death. But God's favor is life in the age to come in Jesus the Messianic King our master.

Paul makes it very clear that *only those who die to sin are vindicated before God.* So what, then, does "dying to sin" mean? Does it mean that sin no longer affects the Christian no matter what he does? Is this how Paul described it? Not even close!

Paul wrote that "dying to sin" means leaving the enslavement to sin to become enslaved to treating other people justly, equitably, and fairly. "Dying to sin" means "becoming a slave to justice."[151] Paul wanted the Mental to understand that only those who die to sin—only those who are slaves to justice—will reap the reward. In fact, Paul concludes this passage by stating that nothing short of total dedication to justice will result in the life of the age to come.

At this point, Paul brings his Jewish readers into the discussion by momentarily referencing a point about the Law:

Romans 7:1-6

Or don't you know, brothers, (**I am now speaking to the ones who know the Law**), that the law rules over someone only as long as he lives? For the married woman is tied, by law, to the husband for as long as he lives. But if the husband happens to die, then she is exempt from the law regarding the husband. Certainly, then, if she becomes another man's while the husband is living, she will be identified as an adulterer. But if the husband should die, she is exempt from the Law, so she will not be an adulterer if she becomes another man's. **For this same reason, my brothers, you also died to the law through the body of the Messianic King in order for you to become another's (to him who was raised from the dead) that we should produce results unto God.**

151 The Koine Greek word *dikaios* referred to "the just, equitable, and fair treatment of others." Paul relies heavily on derivatives of this word throughout Romans chapter six to drive his point home. See Romans in the Latin Vulgate for documentation of this.

> For when we were in the flesh, the interests of sin (the ones via the law) were energized in our members in order to successfully produce results unto death. **But now we are discharged from the Law, having died to that which were tied, in order for us to serve as slaves in newness of spirit, and not the oldness of the written code.**

Paul brings his Jewish readers into the conversation by using the Law to make the same point. He wanted them to understand that they were not freed from the Jobs of the Law in order for them to do whatever they want. Quite the opposite! They were freed from the Jobs of the Law "in order for them to become another's ... in order to serve as slaves."[152] The freedom from the Jobs of the Law was to free them up to be spiritually enslaved to the benevolent treatment of others (which would automatically fulfill the neighbor-based requirements of the old written code).[153] They must *serve as slaves* in the newness of the spirit. What stronger language could Paul have used?

So now, Paul has brought his Jewish readers (the Judaizers) in with the Mental. And now, he's going to explain to both of them what he means about the difference between slavishly serving in "the newness of the spirit" vs. "the oldness of the written code":

> **Romans 7:7-8:4**
>
> **What shall we say then, 'the Law is sin?' No way! On the contrary! For I would not have known about sin if it wasn't for the Law. For example, I wouldn't know about coveting if it wasn't for the Law which said, "Don't covet." But sin seized an opportunity through the commandment by creating in me every possible kind of coveting.** The sin was lifeless without the Law, and I was once alive without the Law. But when the commandment came into my life, sin sprang to life and I died. And the commandment which leads to life proved to be a curse of death to me. For sin seizing an opportunity through the commandment tricked me, and through it killed me. **Therefore the Law is holy (and the commandment holy, fair, and beneficent).**

152 Romans 7:4

153 The *dikaiomata* of the Law were "the Justices of the Law" (the Law's neighbor based commands) according to the Latin Vulgate. (See Romans 2:26, 8:2-4, 13:8-10)

So 'the beneficent thing has become death to me?' No way! But in order for sin to show itself as sin, through the beneficent thing it created death in me, that sin might become exceedingly sinful through the commandment. For we know that the Law is spiritual, but I am made of flesh having been sold to be under sin's control. For I don't understand what I do. For I don't do that which I want to do. Rather that which I consider despicable, this I find myself doing. Now if I am doing the things I don't want to do, then I am agreeing that the Law is an excellent thing. And now is no longer I myself who is doing it, rather it is the sin living in me that is doing it. For I know that nothing beneficient lives in my flesh. Because although the good intentions are present, I do not find myself doing noble things. For I don't do the benevolent things I want to do, rather the malicious things which I don't want to do, this I end up doing. And if I do that which I don't intend to do, then it is no longer me who is doing it, rather it is the sin living in me.

I find then this law: that malice is present in me along with the desire to do noble things. For I joyfully agree with the Law of God in my inner man. But I also see another law in the members of my body, warring against the law of my mind, and taking me captive to the sin's law which is in the members of my body.

What a miserable man I am. Who will rescue me from this body of death? Praise be to God through Jesus the Messianic King our master. So then, I myself indeed slavishly serve the Law of God in my mind, yet serve sin's law in my flesh. **And now there is no condemnation for those in the Messianic King Jesus**—those whose behavior does not conform to the flesh but conforms to the spirit. **For the Law of the spirit of the life in Jesus the Messianic King emancipated me from the Law of sin and death. For what the Law was powerlessness to do (in that it was weakened by the flesh), God did by sending his own son in the likeness of the sinful flesh. And regarding sin he pronounced a sentence on sin in the flesh that the Law's requirement of justice might be fulfilled in us; the ones who don't behave conforming to the flesh be conforming to the spirit.**

Here, Paul explains the difference between serving God based on "the written code" vs. "the newness of the Spirit". He selects *a neighbor-based commandment* ("Do not covet") to make his point.

Most people miss that Paul selected a neighbor-based commandment because they wrongly assume that coveting is a sexual, not ethical, term. Let's see what the word meant in the mid-Koine Christian period.

> Let him of no man covet wife or child,
> His splendid house, his wide-spread property,
> His maiden, or his slave born ill his house,
> His horses, or his cattle, or his adult cows,
> Nay, covet not a pin, O Pamphilus,[154]

To covet a pin meant 'to want another man's pin for yourself,' not to want to have sex with his pin (which would hurt a lot, one would think). The same goes with another man's horses, cattle, and adult cows. "Coveting" meant to want everything for yourself, including what your fellowman has, whether it's his wife, house, cow, or pin.

In short, coveting was the desire for material things over the desire for the well-being of others. In fact, it was even possible to covet your own belongings (if you desired to hold onto them over using them for the welfare of others). When the second century church father Irenaeus was commenting on the rich man who refused Jesus' command to sell his possessions and give to the poor, he wrote:

> the Lord, **exposing his covetousness,** said to him, "If thou wilt be perfect, go, sell all that thou hast, and distribute to the poor; and come, follow me;" promising to those who would act thus, the portion belonging to the apostles.[155]

Irenaeus called the man "covetous" because he valued his own material possessions more than the needs of his fellowman.[156] This is the heart of coveting. **Coveting is the exact opposite of loving other people just as much as you love yourself and that's why the apostle Paul used it as his example in Romans chapter seven.**

So now that we understand what coveting meant in the Koine Greek period, we're ready to explore Paul's use of that word.

First, Paul emphasizes that the written neighbor-based commands, such as "Do not covet", were meant to bring an awareness to sin. It's commandments based on loving your neighbor as yourself

154 Second Century Christian writing: *On the Sole Government of God* by Justin Martyr, chapter IV (as found in *ANF01. The Apostolic Fathers with Justin Martyr and Irenaeus* by Philip Schaff)

155 "Against Heresies: Book IV" by Irenaeus, chapter twelve, paragraph five

156 See also Ignatius's exhortation against those who are "covetous of other men's possessions, swallowing up wealth insatiably." (*Espistle to the Magnesians* by Saint Ignatius, chapter IX). Ignatius was a contemporary of the apostles and studied under Jesus' disciple, John.

which were meant to bring an awareness of sin.

Second, Paul said that the awareness gained through the written neighbor-based requirements—through the written code—only made matters worse for him. Now that the written code made him aware of coveting, his awareness became focused on his own coveting. And the more he became aware of his own coveting, the more he coveted. In fact, it got to the point where Paul experienced "every possible kind of coveting." The neighbor-based commands in the written code ended up producing death instead of life. The written code was powerless to enable Paul to live up to the neighbor-based commands.

Third, Paul explains that this is the very reason why Jesus of Nazareth sacrificed his life. In Paul's theology, Jesus' sacrifice allowed for "the Law of the spirit of life to emancipate him from the Law of sin and death." What is the spirit's role in all of this? "The Law's requirement of justice (the Law's requirement to treat others justly, equitably, and fairly) is totally fulfilled in those who behave according to the spirit." The written code couldn't get people to treat their fellowman equitably. So God sent Jesus as a sacrifice in order to send the spirit to empower people to finally fulfill the neighbor-based commands in their daily lives.

Romans 8:5-17

For the ones who conform to the flesh think fleshly things. But the ones conforming to the spirit think spiritual things. For the mind set on the flesh is death, but the mind set on the spirit is life and peace. **Because the mind set on the flesh is hostile to God because it doesn't submit itself to the authority of the Law of God nor is it able to do so.** And the ones who conform to the flesh are unable to please God. But you are not in the flesh, but in the spirit, if indeed the spirit of God inhabits you. But if anyone doesn't have the spirit of the Messianic King, he is not one of his.

But if Messianic King is in you, indeed the body is dead via sin, but the spirit lives via equitableness. And if the spirit of the one raising Jesus from the dead lives in you, the one who raised the Messianic King from the dead shall give life also to your mortal bodies via his spirit in you. Therefore, then, brothers, we are obligated not to the flesh, to behave conforming to it. **For if your behavior conforms to the flesh then you are going to die. But if in the spirit you put to death the behavior of the body then you shall live. For only those who are conducted by the spirit of God are sons of God.** For you didn't receive a spirit of slavish servitude again unto fear, but you received a spirit of adoption in which we cry out Abba, father. The spirit himself bears witness with our spirit that we are children of God. And if we are children, then we are also God's heirs (coheirs of the Messianic King) provided we suffer the same thing as him in order that we also should share the same glory as well.

It is here that Paul gives the Mental their ultimate smack down. He assures them that *if their behavior conforms to the flesh, then they are going to die.* Period. So much for increasing the favor by sinning!

But what exactly is the opposite of "conforming to the flesh?" What must a person do to live?

> **Therefore don't let sin rule in your mortal body, obeying it in what it wants. Nor offer the members of your body to as tools of injustice. But offer yourselves to God as one living out of the dead, and your members to God as tools of justice.**[157]

157 Romans 6:12-13. Paul contrasts *adikia* (the unjust treatment of others) against *dikaiosunes* (justice, equity, and fairness). See the Latin Vulgate for the meaning of these important words used in Romans 6:12-13

For Paul, sin reigning in the mortal body (i.e. sin reigning the flesh) is a euphemism for "offering the members of your body as tools of injustice." In Romans chapter three Paul discussed those whose *feet* were swift to shed blood, whose *lips* were full of poison, and whose *throats* were an open tomb. These folks, who lacked loving kindness, were using the members of their body as instruments of injustice. *This is Paul's view of what sin reigning in the flesh looks like.* Modern conservative Christianity has sexualized the phrase in direct contradiction to what Paul wrote.[158] In doing so, it has missed Paul's ethical point entirely.

Paul's remedy was to stop using the members of the body as tools of injustice, and instead, to offer the members as instruments of justice unto God. Through benevolent actions, Christians are to be the hands of God and feet of God. What does Paul say will happen to the Christian who doesn't fulfill the neighbor-based commands through the empowerment of the spirit?

> Therefore, then, brothers, we are obligated not to the flesh, to behave conforming to it. **For if your behavior conforms to the flesh then you are going to die.** But if in the spirit you put to death the behavior of the body then you shall live. For only those who are conducted by the spirit of God are sons of God.[159]

Paul assures the Mental that if their behavior conforms to the flesh—if they continue to use the members of their body as instruments of injustice—they are going to die. Paul assured them that any Christian who continues to treat his fellowman inequitably will perish. Period.

158 As the Latin Vulgate attests

159 Romans 8:12-14

Summary

The Mental: These folks thought that all their sins (past, present, and future) were covered over based on what they mentally believed.

The Smack Down: Paul told them to make no mistake about it: If they continued to treat their fellowman unjustly, then they are going to die. Period.

Counter Points: Paul clarified that "being free from sin" was not a license to sin. On the contrary, it meant "to be enslaved to justice." The Mental got the meaning wrong, and so Paul set them straight.

The very reason that Jesus came was to empower Christians to fulfill all the neighbor-based commands via his spirit living in them. Only those who conform to the spirit—only those who keep the neighbor-based commands—are vindicated before God. Everyone else is rejecting the purpose for which Jesus came and will suffer the appropriate consequences for doing so.

Chapter 28
The Predestined Proud

The final group that Paul addresses in his letter is the Predestined Proud.

> But if some of the branches were cut off, and you a wild olive tree were grafted in to share in the root and of the sap of the olive tree, don't gloat over the branches!... For I don't want you to be ignorant, brothers, of the following secret knowledge (in order for you not to be conceited)[160]

The Predestined Proud were gloating over the idea that Israelites were predestined to be cut off in order for them (the chosen Gentiles) to be grafted in. We find that Paul is less than pleased with their gloating and conceit. So let's find out how Paul knocked the Predestined Proud down a couple of notches:

160 Romans 11:17, 25

Romans 8:18-39

For I reckon the sufferings of the present time aren't even worthy of comparison to the glory that is going to be disclosed to us. **For in eager expectation the creation anxiously awaits the disclosure of the sons of God. For creation was submitted to purposelessness, not willingly, but through the one submitting it, in hope that the creation itself shall be emancipated from the slavery of mortality into the immortal freedom of the glory of the children of God.** For we are well informed that the entire creation has groaned together in its shared pain up until the present time. And not only it, but also us who have the first fruit of the spirit, even we ourselves groan within ourselves **anxiously awaiting adoption—the rescue of our body.**

For in hope we were saved. But hope which is seen is no hope at all, for who hopes for what he already sees? But if we hope for what we do not see then by perseverance we excitedly await. And likewise also the spirit helps us in our limitations. For the things we need to pray for we do not always know, but the spirit itself takes over on our behalf with unspeakable groans. And the one searching the hearts knows the thoughts of the spirit because its pleadings for the holy ones accords with God. And we are well informed that to those who love God everything works together for the benefit of those being invited according to purpose. **For those he foreknew, he also predetermined to have a similar form to the likeness of his son so that he would be the first one born out of many brothers. And those he predetermined, these are the ones he also invited. And those he invited, these he also vindicated. And these he vindicated, these he also made glorious.**

What then shall we say to such things? If God is for us, who can be against us? He who indeed didn't spare his own son, but handed him over for the sake of us all, will he not also grant all things to us with him? **Who can enter a charge against the invited of God? For God is the one vindicating.** So who can possibly condemn? Messianic King who died (and more importantly was raised from the dead and is also at the right hand of God) makes an appeal in person for us. And who can separate us from the love of the Messianic King? Shall pain, or troubles, or persecution, or famine, or destitution, or danger, or sword? As it was written, "On account of you we are being put to death all day long. They consider us sheep to be slaughtered." But in all of this we completely prevail through the one who loved us. **For I am convinced that neither death, nor life, nor angels, nor magistrates, nor things present, nor things to come, nor height, nor depth, nor anything else created will be able to separate us from the love of God which is in Jesus the Messianic King our master.**

Paul's setup is absolutely brilliant. It cannot be emphasized enough that Romans 8:18-11:36 is one long continuous passage (dealing with one overarching issue). The passage takes many turns, only to end with a very surprising twist. If you keep your eye on the flow from beginning to end, you will find that Paul has crafted one of the most brilliant essays found in the entire Bible.

Now the excerpt above was Paul's introduction to the larger passage. It accomplishes quite a few things.

First, it foreshadows the surprise ending. Paul writes that the whole creation was forced (not by choice) into purposelessness by God. Paul says that God did this "in hope that the creation itself shall be emancipated from the slavery of mortality into the immortal freedom of the glory of the children of God." Chances are that Paul believes God always gets the things he hopes for (as will become evident as the passage progresses). But for now, we have the hope that predestination is a plan for the children of God to be revealed in order that they might somehow bring immortality to the rest of creation. (The rest of the protracted discussion rests on this foundation.)

Second, the passage places "the adoption" into the future, as a yet unaccomplished event. This reminder that the Christians' "rescue of the body" hasn't yet happened will come into play as the passage progresses.

Third, Paul brilliantly intertwines both free will and fate: "For those he foreknew, he also predetermined." The first century Pharisees believed in the interplay between fate and free will. Paul is letting his readers know that he does too. With these three things, the setup for the rest of the passage is complete:

The Setup

1. God predestined creation to purposelessness "in hope" that creation might somehow be freed from the shackles of mortality into the immortal freedom of the predestined children of God.
2. The Christians' adoption—the rescue of their body—is still a future event.
3. The foreknowledge of individual choices is intertwined with predestination. (There is interplay between freewill and fate.)

So let's now dive into the next part of the passage:

Romans 9:1-15

I am speaking what is true in the Messianic King. I am not lying (my conscience testifies along with me in the Holy Spirit) that I am grieved, and continually distressed in my heart because I wish I could be cursed away from the Messianic King for the sake of my brothers, my kin according to flesh; those who are Israelites, to whom belongs the adoption, and the majesty, and the covenants, and the collective law, and the worship of God, and the promises, from who are the fathers, and from whom is the Messianic King according to flesh who is over all—God praised throughout the ages. Amen.

But it's not as though the word of God has run aground; for they are not all Israel who are from Israel; neither are they all children who are Abraham's descendents; but in Isaac your descendents will be called to you. That is to say, it is not the children of the flesh who are children of God; but the children of the promise are considered descendents. For this is how the promise was stated, "At this time I will come and Sarah will have a son." And not only this, but also there's also Rebecca who conceived twins by one man—Isaac our father. **And while they were still unborn, before they had done anything helpful or malicious, that the plan of God according to selection would remain not from deeds but from the one who does the inviting it was said to her, "The older shall serve the younger." As it has been written, "Jacob I loved, but Esau I loved less."**

> **What shall we say then? 'There isn't any injustice with God?' No way! For to Moses he said, "I will show mercy on whomever I should show mercy, and I shall have compassion on whomever I should have compassion."** So it is not the one who wants it, nor is it the one who tries, instead it's the one God has mercy on. For the scriptures says, to Pharaoh, "This is why I raised you up: so that I could demonstrate my power in you, so that my name would be declared in all the land." **So he has compassion on whomever he wants and he hardens the heart of whomever he wants.**

The Jewish scriptures promised that all of Israel will have a share in the life of the age to come—the life of the Messianic Age. So Paul tells his readers that, as far as this particular promise is concerned, not every natural-born Israelite is 'Israel.' He further states that those who are chosen to 'be Israel' are indeed predestined. He goes further still to say that God prevents some people from becoming Israel. In Paul's theology, God even goes so far as to harden the hearts of whomever he wants, to make sure they don't turn to him and have life in the age to come.

So is this it? Is this where the passage ends? No way! Keep the last sentence of the section above in mind as you make your way to the end of the passage: "God has compassion on whomever he wants and he hardens the heart of whomever he wants." Like any good mystery writer, Paul has just set the reader up for a very big surprise:

Romans 9:19-33

Then you will say to me, 'Why then does he blame people? For who can resist his will?' Excuse me? Who are you to talk back to God? Shall that which is molded say to the molder, "Why did you make me like this?" Or does the potter not have the freedom to choose, from out of the same batch of clay, to make one jar for privileged use, and the other jar for shameful use? And if God wanting to demonstrate his wrath and reveal his capability put up with much patience jars of wrath created for destruction; and to reveal the abundance of his majesty upon jars of compassion which he created beforehand for majesty, who also he invited not only from out of Jews but also from out of nations as he also says in Hosea, "I will call those who are not my people, 'my people,' and he who was not beloved, 'beloved.' And it will be in that place where it was said to them, 'you are not my people,' there they shall be called sons of the living God." And Isaiah cries concerning Israel, "Though the number of the sons of Israel should be as the sand of the sea, a small portion shall be saved. For the master will accomplish his word over the land completely and abruptly."

And just as Isaiah foretold, "If the Lord of the Sabbath didn't leave a handful of descendents for us we would have become like Sodom and like Gomorrah." **What shall we say then? That Gentiles who didn't pursue justice, attained justice—the justice which comes out of faith. But Israel, pursuing a law of justice, never made it to a law of justice. Why? Because they didn't approach it by faith, but instead approached it as if it were out of the Jobs of the Law.** For they tripped over the tripping stone just as it was written, "Behold I lay in Zion a stone which people will trip over, and a rock which will ensnare; but everyone who has faith in him won't be sorry."

In this part, Paul conflates God's ability to choose whomever he wants with Israel's own poor choices—their poor approach to the Law. Most Jews couldn't have faith in Jesus' interpretation of the Law because they were blinded by the Jobs of the Law. They were so convinced that the Jobs of the Law were necessary that they refused to believe in what Jesus taught. However, Jesus' message made perfect sense to the Gentiles—those who were never pursuing a law of justice in the first place. The idea of a God who only desires for them to care for each other rang true, and so they placed their faith in Jesus. Thus, because of the Jobs of the Law, the Jews tripped over the tripping stone:

Romans 10:1-17

Brothers, indeed the good-will of my heart and my prayer to God for Israel is for their salvation. For I attest that they are zealous for God, but not according to knowledge. For in their ignorance of the justice of God they sought to establish their own justice (not submitting themselves to the justice of God). For the Messianic King is the completeness of the Law unto justice for everyone who believes. For Moses writes about the justice, the one out of Law, that, "The man who practices them shall live in them." But of the justice of faith therefore he says, "You should not say in your heart, 'Who will ascend into heaven?' That is to bring the Messianic King down; or, 'Who will descend into the Netherworld?' That is to bring the Messianic King out of the dead. But what does it say? "The word is near you, in your mouth and in your heart," that is the word of faith we publicly proclaim: **that if you solemnly pledge with your mouth Jesus is your master, and believe in your heart that God raised him from the dead, you will be saved.** For the heart believes unto justice, and the mouth solemnly pledges unto salvation. For the scripture says, "Everyone who trusts him will not be sorry." And there is no difference between the Jews and Greeks; for the same master of all is generous to everyone making an appeal to him. "For whoever makes an appeal in the name of the master will be saved."

How then can they make an appeal to someone they have not trusted? And how can they trust in someone they have not heard of? And how can they hear unless someone makes him known? And how can anyone make him known unless he is sent? Just as it was written, "How beautiful are the feet of those announcing good news of beneficence." But not everyone obeyed the good news; for Isaiah says, "O Lord, who had faith in our report?" **So the faith comes out of hearing, and the hearing through Messianic King's statement."**

The Gentile's faith came from them hearing the "Messianic King's statement" (the Golden Rule).[161] The moment they believed the statement, they pledged to make Jesus the master of their lives and they were saved from the consequences of their previously committed sins.[162]

161 According to James 1:21-25, 2:8 the word that saves is the King's Law, which concurs with the scripture, "Love your neighbor as yourself." In other words, it's the Golden Rule. Paul would have taught the same word that saves as James did.

162 Paul has already specified that it's the previously committed sins that are passed over the moment a person believes. See the previous discussion on the Judaizers.

Romans 10:18-11:10

But I say, 'Didn't they hear?' Of course, for their voice went to all the land, and their declarations to the ends of the inhabited world. But I say, 'Didn't Israel know?' First Moses told them, "I will make you jealous over those who are not a nation; by an ignorant people I will make you angry." And Isaiah was very bold, and said, "I was found by those who were not looking for me; I became known to those who weren't even asking for me." **But to Israel he said, "All day long I hold out my hands to a disobedient and stubborn people."**

I say then, 'Did God push his people out of the way?' No way! For I too am an Israelite, a descendant of Abraham, of the tribe of Benjamin. **God didn't push away people whom he foreknew.** Or don't you know what Elijah says in the scripture, how he personally appealed to God regarding Israel, saying, "O Master, they murdered your prophets and tore down your altars, and I am the only one left, and they seek to end my life." But what was the divine response to him?" I have set aside seven thousand men for myself, those who haven't bowed to Baal." **In the same way there has come about in the present time a handful according to a favored selection. And if it is by a favor, then it is no longer through jobs, otherwise the favor is no longer a favor. And if it is by jobs, then it is no longer a favor, otherwise the jobs are no longer a job. So what then? What Israel searched for, this it did not obtain; rather those who were selected obtained it, and the rest who were not selected were made blind.** Just as it was written, "God gave to them a spirit of unconsciousness, of eyes that don't see, and ears which don't hear," up until this very day. And David says, "Let their table become a trap and a net to ensnare them and a booby trap to repay them. Let their eyes be darkened so they cannot see and their backs completely bent backwards."

Once again, we find the interplay between predestination and foreknowledge, for Paul writes, "God didn't push away people he foreknew." According to Paul, God foreknew that Israel would reject Jesus' teaching so he decided to blind all but a handful of them. God further chose to select some Gentiles to take the place of the blinded Jews. (The Gentiles would be included without any obligation to the Jobs of the Law; otherwise, the selection couldn't rightly be considered a favor.)

Romans 11:11-24

I say then, 'Were they made to trip in order to make them fall?' No way! Rather their wrongdoing is salvation to the Gentiles in order to make them jealous. Now if their wrongdoing is wealth to the world and their loss is wealth to the Gentiles, how much more shall the fulfillment of them be? For I speak to you Gentiles. In as much as I am an apostle of the Gentiles I honor my service, if somehow I make my countrymen jealous and save some of them. For if their rejection is the reconciliation of the world, what else would their acceptance be other than life from the dead. And if the first lump is holy, so also is the whole batch; and if the root is holy, then so also are the branches.

But if some of the branches were cut off, and you a wild olive tree were grafted in to share in the root and of the sap of the olive tree, don't gloat over the branches! You who are gloating don't support the root. Rather the root supports you. So you will say then, "The branches were cut off so that I could be grafted in." Without a doubt! They were cut off because of their distrust and you were established by your trust. **You shouldn't be cocky, but afraid. For if God didn't spare the natural branches he won't spare you either.**

Witness the kindness and severity of God! To those who fell—severity; yet to you—kindness (if you persist in kindness otherwise you also will be cut off). And they also, if they stop persisting in distrust, they shall be grafted in (for God is able to graft them in again). For if you were cut off from nature's wild olive tree, and contrary to nature were grafted into the refined olive tree, how much more shall these be grafted into their own natural olive tree?

Here, Paul reveals his belief that God had a specific purpose in making the Jews trip. The Jews were made to trip in order to bring salvation to the Gentiles. The vast majority of Jews were cut off so that many Gentiles could be grafted in. Some of the Gentiles were apparently gloating over the idea. So Paul gave them a stern warning. He warned them that just because they were predestined to be grafted in, doesn't mean that they can't be cut right back out. In fact, if they cease showing other people the same kindness that God had showed to them, then they most assuredly would be cut out. Likewise, if the blinded Jews should happen to change their ways, they too could be grafted right back in.

Apparently, the predestination isn't set in stone (due to the interplay with freewill). And now, Paul has set the reader up for the grand finale—the ultimate twist:

> **Romans 11:25-36**
>
> **For I don't want you to be ignorant, brothers, of the following secret knowledge (in order for you not to be conceited): the blindness on part of Israel has come about only until the fullness of the Gentiles enters in, and in this manner all Israel will be saved.** Just as it is written, "The rescuer shall come from out of Zion, and he shall take away the Godless deeds from Jacob. And this is the covenant to them by me, when I take away their sins."
>
> In regard to the gospel they have become detested for your sake, but in regards to the selection beloved for the sake of the fathers. **For the favors and the selection of God are not to be regretted: For just as you chosen ones once disobeyed God but now have been shown mercy because of the blinded ones' disobedience; so also the blinded ones who are now disobedient will be shown mercy because of the mercy shown to you chosen ones. For God imprisoned everyone in disobedience in order for him to show mercy to everyone.** O how deep is God's wealth and wisdom and knowledge. How as unfathomable are his decisions and incomprehensible are his ways. For "who has known the mind of the Master, or whoever became his adviser?" Or "whoever first gave to him that he should be obligated to repay him?" For from out of him, and through him and unto him are all things. To him be the majesty throughout the ages. Amen.

Surprise! There is some secret knowledge that the Predestined Proud didn't know about: The blindness on Israel is only temporary and "*in this manner* all Israel will be saved." Because the blindness is temporary, all Israel will be saved.

Paul reveals that God will grant two favors[163]: one to the selected Gentiles and one to the blinded Jews. Just as the selected Gentiles once disobeyed and were shown mercy because of the blinded Jews' disobedience, so the blinded Jews will also be shown mercy because of the mercy shown to the selected Gentiles. God predestined the disobedience of everyone so that he might have mercy on everyone.

163 The Koine Greek text specifies favors (plural)

Surprise … God has predestined the reconciliation of the entire world, so stop gloating.[164]

This is why the passage must be read from beginning to end. Too many people stop when they read: "God has compassion on whomever he wants and he hardens the heart of whomever he wants." But that statement was part of a larger message:

> **"I will show mercy on whomever I should show mercy**, and I shall have compassion on whomever I should have compassion."… For God imprisoned everyone in disobedience **in order for him to show mercy to everyone.**

Paul was setting up the surprise ending. Yes, God will have mercy on whomever he wants … and he has chosen to ultimately have mercy on absolutely everyone.

Did you happen to notice how the surprise perfectly aligns with the very beginning of the passage?

> For in eager expectation the creation anxiously awaits the disclosure of the sons of God. For creation was submitted to purposelessness, not willingly, but through the one submitting it, **in hope that the creation itself shall be emancipated from the slavery of mortality into the immortal freedom of the glory of the children of God**….
>
> For the favors and the selection of God are not to be regretted: **For just as you chosen ones once disobeyed God but now have been shown mercy because of the blinded ones' disobedience; so also the blinded ones who are now disobedient will be shown mercy because of the mercy shown to you chosen ones.** For God imprisoned everyone in disobedience in order for him to show mercy to everyone.

Paul foreshadowed the ending when he wrote that God predestined creation into purposelessness, hoping that it would result in all of creation being freed from the shackles of mortality. Paul foreshadowed a two-step process: first, the children of God (the chosen ones) would be revealed, and then (God hoped) all of creation would subsequently be emancipated into the same immortal freedom as the chosen ones.

164 See Appendix B, "The Stages of the Ages," for more details.

Not too surprisingly, Paul ends the passage with God getting what he hoped for. In Paul's theology, the mercy shown to the chosen ones gives God the freedom to show the same mercy to the blinded ones.[165] All of creation is liberated into the freedom of the children of God, so that God can be all in all.

Summary

The Predestined Proud: These folks were conceitedly gloating over the idea that natural-born Israelites were predestined to be cut off in order for them to be grafted in.

The Smack Down: Just because you have been predestined to be grafted in doesn't mean that you can't be cut right back out. In fact, if you don't show others the same kindness that God has shown you, then you most assuredly will be cut off.

Counterpoints: Israel's predestined blindness didn't happen in order to cast them away forever. Rather, the predestined plan was set in motion to ultimately cause everyone to be reconciled to God.

Even more so, God is going to have mercy on the blinded Jews because of the mercy he has shown to you.

You are going to share eternity with these folks, so stop gloating.

165 See Appendix B, "The Stages of the Ages," for a discussion on the Old Testament's prophecy that God will have mercy on the disobedient because of the mercy he shows to the chosen ones.

Chapter 29
The Conclusion

Prior to the twentieth century, scholars didn't possess even one original first century Koine Greek writing; not one. However, at the turn of the twentieth century, a treasure trove of Koine Greek papyri was discovered buried in the sands of Egypt. There were so many papyri that the bulk of material was measured in the tons when it was shipped to London for analysis. Overnight, the world went from having none to having literally tons of Koine papyri. And Biblical scholarship has never been the same since.

Among the multitude of new findings was the discovery of a standard Hellenistic letter format. Virtually all the letters discovered had an identical format. It didn't matter if the letter was written by someone rich or poor; each letter had the same format. It didn't matter if the letter was written for business or personal reasons; each letter had the same format.

The basic format is as follows:

- **Greetings**—The start of the letter not only included saying 'hello,' but was very positively stated (even if the letter would later contain criticism). This explains how Paul instantly switches from his flowery greeting at the beginning of the letter into his scathing criticism. The beginning of the letter was a formulaic positive greeting consistent with the letters of the time period.

- **The body**—The body explained why the letter was written in the first place.
- **Conclusion and Salutations**—Letters written to more than one person (especially longer letters) included a concluding section before the salutations (because these letters were often meant to be read aloud). The writer would often spend a lot of time making sure that the conclusion (the part the listener was more likely to remember) contained the 'take away' information. And the concluding section of Paul's letter to the Romans was very rich in 'take away' information.

As we explore the concluding section of Paul's letter, keep in mind that he likely considered this to contain some of the most important information. As you will soon see, Paul uses the concluding section to offer a single remedy that was applicable to all four groups: the Hypocrites, the Judaizers, the Mental, and the Predestined Proud. Paul would offer a single remedy that would resolve all four issues in one fell swoop.

Without further adieu, let's examine the first part of the conclusion (which is now addressing everyone in Rome):

Romans 12:1-8

So I urge you, brothers, through the kindnesses of God, to put your bodies at his disposal as living, dedicated sacrifices acceptable to God as your thoughtful worship. And don't be conformed to this age, but be transformed by renewing your mind so you can ascertain what God's will is; that which is benevolent, acceptable and perfectly complete. For I say through the favor being given to me, to everyone among you, **don't consider yourselves too highly, above what you must think; but to be level headed; as God has appointed to each person a measure of faith.**

> For just as our one body has many members which do not have the same function, so too we who form one body in the Messianic King are each other's members. But we have different bestowments according to that which has been bestowed upon us: if prophecy, its according to the proportion of faith; if service, it according to the service; if teaching, its according to the instruction; it comforting, its according to the comfort; if sharing, its according to generosity; if taking care of others, its according to willingness; if it's being merciful to others, its according to graciousness.

The first thing that Paul does is tell everyone to be living sacrifices, totally dedicated to the service of God, and to accept all the members of the church as equal to themselves—regardless of the function or amount of faith a person may have.

> **Romans 12:9-21**
>
> **Love each other sincerely. Abhor worthlessness. Cling to benevolence, dearly loving one another with brotherly love.** Mutually guide each other in respect—not being lazy in your diligence, but with an enthusiastic spirit slavishly serve the master: rejoicing in hope, enduring suffering, devoted to prayer, constantly attending to the needs of the holy ones. Pursue hospitality. **Praise those who persecute you. Praise and do not curse.**
>
> **Rejoice with those who are rejoicing. And weep with those who are weeping. Don't show favoritism. Don't be conceited but befriend the less fortunate.** Don't consider yourselves to be above reproach. **Never repay malice with malice.** Take consideration of what is beautiful in the eyes of all men. If possible, as much as comes from your part, keep the peace with all men. Never avenge yourself, beloved, but give room for wrath. For just as it was written, "Vengeance is mine. I will repay," says the Master. Rather, **"if then your enemy is hungry, feed him! If he is thirsty, give him a drink! For in doing this you shall heap burning coals upon his head."** **Don't be conquered by malice, but conquer malice with benevolence.**

Once again, Paul calls the Roman Christians to brotherly love, a brotherly love that empathizes with others: "Rejoice with those who are rejoicing. And weep with those who are weeping." It is a brotherly love that considers everyone equal to themselves, including the less fortunate. It is a brotherly love that even extends to enemies.

Paul quoted Proverbs 25:21-22 in the passage above:

> If your enemy is hungry, give him food to eat;
> And if he is thirsty, give him water to drink;
> For you will heap burning coals on his head,
> **And the LORD will reward you.**

Paul was reminding his readers that they will only reap God's reward if they love everyone ... even their enemies.

> **Romans 13:1-7**
>
> **Everyone should submit themselves to the ruling authorities.** For there is no authority unless it comes from God; those authorities that exist are established by God. Therefore whoever resists the government resists the edict of God. And those who oppose will receive judgment upon themselves. **For the rulers are not to be feared by those who do benevolent deeds, but those who are malicious.**
>
> **Do you want to have no fear of the government? Then do benevolent things and you will even have its praise. For it is an agent of God to you for benevolence. But if you do malicious things, then fear! For it doesn't wear the sword for no reason. For it is an agent of God, avenging unto wrath those who do malicious things.** Therefore it is absolutely necessary to submit yourselves, not only because of the wrath, but also for the sake of your own conscience. For this reason, also pay your taxes in full. For they are God's assistants, constantly attending this very thing. Give everyone their due: to the one who taxes—the tax; to the one who imposes duties—the duty; to the one commanding respect—the respect; to the one commanding honor—the honor.

Love of others, expressed through benevolence, is so strong in Paul's mind that even his call to submit to the authorities is based upon it. Since governments themselves applaud those who do benevolent things, then governments themselves are agents of God (so goes the reasoning of Paul). Paul so badly wants for benevolence to be the 'take away' that he wraps it around every point he makes in the conclusion—even his discussion on submitting to the government.

> **Romans 13:8-14**
>
> **Owe nothing to anyone other than to love them because love of others fulfills the entire Law. For "don't be unfaithful," "don't murder," "don't steal," "don't covet," and if there's any other commandment, it is recapitulated in this statement: "Love your neighbor as yourself." Love of neighbor does nothing malicious. Therefore such love then is the fulfillment of the entire Law.**
>
> Do this knowing the time: that it is already the hour for you to wake up from your sleep. For now salvation is nearer to us than when we first believed. The night is almost over, and the day is drawing near. Therefore let's take off the deeds of darkness, and put on the armory of light. **Let's behave decently as during the day, not in excessive feasting and drunkenness; not in screwing around and licentiousness; not in quarrels and jealousy. But clothe yourselves in master Jesus, the Messianic King. And don't spend time thinking how to satisfy the wants of the flesh.**

And now, Paul hits the nail right on the head. He reminds the Roman Christians that brotherly love is their one obligation *because that's what fulfills the Law.* (An obligation 'because of the Law' is an obligation 'to the Law.') The Christian's one obligation is to the Messianic King's interpretation of the Law—the Law comprised of all the commandments recapitulated in the statement, "Love your neighbor as yourself."

It's also important to note how Paul lumps together excessive feasting, drunkenness, screwing around, licentiousness, quarrels and jealousy. These are all selfish things that result from trying to satisfy what the flesh wants. Too often, Paul's discussions on 'the flesh' get spun as exclusively referring to sexual pursuits. But in the body of Romans, Paul equated all forms of injustice against others as examples of doing what the flesh wants. And now, in the conclusion, he equates all forms of selfish living with satisfying the flesh, as well. To Paul, all selfishness and injustice come from 'the flesh,' and all love and equitableness come from 'the spirit.' It's time for Paul's terminology to be embraced for what it is, not spun into something else to promote certain doctrinal ideas.

Romans 14:1-15:7

Befriend the one who is weak in the faith and don't dispute his opinions. The person strong in faith eats all things, but the one who is weak eats only vegetables. The one who eats everything is not to disdain the one who doesn't. And the one who doesn't eat everything is not to pass judgment on the one who does—for God has accepted him. Who are you to pass judgment on another's servant? To his own master he stands or falls. And he will stand because God is able to make him stand.

One person considers one day more important than the others. Another considers every day to be the same. Let each be fully convinced in his own mind. The one intent on the day, it is for the Master that he is intent. And the one not intent on the day, it is for the master that he is not intent. The one who eats everything, it is for the master that he eats and gives thanks to God. And the one who doesn't eat everything, it is for the master that he doesn't eat and gives thanks to God. For none of us lives to himself and none of us dies to himself. For both, if we should live, we should live to the master. And if we die, it is for the master we should die. So that whether we live or die we are the master's. For this reason the Messianic King both died and lived: that he might be master over both the dead and the living.

But you, why do you pass judgment on your brother? Or why do you also disdain your brother? For all of us will be brought before the tribunal of God. Just as it was written, "As surely as I live, says the Master, every knee shall bow to me and every tongue make a confession to God." **Therefore let's not judge one another but rather determine to do this—to not put an obstacle or trap in front of a brother's path. I am well informed and firmly convinced in the master Jesus, that nothing is profane in itself.** Only to him who thinks something is profane is it profane.

But if you upset your brother over food, you are no longer walking according to love. Don't use your food to destroy him for whom the Messianic King died. Therefore, don't let your benevolence be maligned. **For the kingdom of God isn't about food and drink, but equitableness, peace and joy in the Holy Spirit. For he who slavishly serves the Messianic King, this way is acceptable to God and esteemed by men; which is why you should pursue the things of peace and the things which build others up.**

Don't destroy the work of God because of food. All things are pure, but they become malicious to the man who eats and causes his brother to stumble. It is ideal to not eat meat and not drink wine nor do anything which causes your brother to stumble. The faith you have, keep it between you and God. **Happy is the man who doesn't judge himself over what he approves.** But he who judges himself is condemned if he eats because his eating is not out of faith. And everything that is not out of faith is missing the mark.

Now we who are strong should bear the weaknesses of those who are weak, and not just seek our own pleasure. Each of us is to please his neighbor for his benefit and to build him up. For even the Messianic King didn't seek to please himself. Just as it was written, "The insults of those mocking you fell on me." For whatever was written previously was written for our instruction, that through perseverance and through the encouragement unify your minds in accordance with the Messianic King Jesus. That with one mind, in one voice you should praise the God and father of our Master Jesus the Messianic King. Therefore, accept one another just as the Messianic King accepted us unto the praise of God.

This section is rather quite interesting. Here, Paul labels the liberal Christian as the man of faith and the conservative Christian as the one who is weak in faith. The liberal Christian understands that nothing else matters other than loving your neighbor as yourself. Reaching such an understanding is to have total faith in what Jesus taught. But conservative Christians genuinely have a hard time believing that this is all that matters. They truly believe that God still insists on religious rules and regulations. So Paul calls upon the liberal Christians to lovingly allow the conservatives to keep their rules and regulations.

But it's vitally important to make a distinction between a Christian who believes in additional rules vs. people who believe they are Christians while not embracing the very foundation of Christianity—the Golden Rule. For example, a Christian can embrace the Golden Rule, but he can also believe in not eating meat. Or he may embrace the Golden Rule, but also believe that God wants him to make one day of the week more special than another.

Paul's premise is that, as long as they are following the Golden Rule, then it's okay for them to keep their rules and regulations. Yet, none of this negates Paul's previous stern warnings against those who think they are Christians while breaking the Golden Rule. Such folks are not brothers in Christ. As a reminder, Paul quite specifically warned such folks that:

- They shall not escape God's equitable judgment, which will be based on the benevolence of their deeds.[166]
- Only the doers of the Law will be vindicated before God.[167]
- Religious rules and regulations (such as the Jobs of the Law) do not vindicate a person before God.[168]
- Only those who keep the neighbor-based commands through the power of the spirit will be vindicated before God.[169]
- If they do not keep the neighbor-based commands through the power of the spirit, they are going to die.[170]
- If they do not show others the same kindness that God has shown to them, they will be cut off.[171]

166 Romans 2:3-11
167 Romans 2:13
168 Romans 3:20
169 Romans 8:3-4
170 Romans 8:13
171 Romans 11:22

All these warnings were issued in the body of the letter. So the presumption in the concluding section is that Paul is speaking of Christian brothers (those who embrace the Golden Rule) but don't have enough faith to understand that this is all that God wants from them.

The same is true today. If conservative Christianity can at least embrace the necessity of the Golden Rule, then liberal Christians are called to allow them to imbibe additional rules and regulations—provided they've truly embraced the foundation. For not everyone will reach a completeness of faith in this life, where they realize that loving others is truly the one and only thing God wants from them.

Chapter 30
Salutations

After the concluding remarks are over, Paul instantly switches into formulaic salutations mode. The flowery Paul seems to spring out of nowhere (but the Koine papyri inform us of the reason behind the shift). After warning each of the four groups that they are all destined for God's wrath, unless they begin loving each other as themselves, he begins praising them again in the salutary process:

> **Romans 15:8-33**
>
> But I say, Messianic King Jesus has become an agent of the descendents of Abraham for the sake of the truth to prove the reliability of the promises given to the fathers, and the nations, to praise God on account of his clemency. Just as it was written, "Because of this I will make acknowledgement of you among the nations, and to your name I will strum." And again it says, "Be glad, O nations, with his people!" And again, "Praise the Lord, all the nations, and praise him all peoples!" And again Isaiah says, "There will be the root of Jesse, and the one rising up to rule nations, upon him nations shall hope." And the God of hope, may he fill you with all joy and peace in trusting, for you abounding in the hope, in power of holy spirit.

And I myself am convinced, my brothers, concerning you, that you yourselves also are full of benevolence, having been filled with all knowledge, fully capable also to counsel one another; and I wrote you more boldly on some parts, brothers, to remind you, because of the favor given to me by God. For I am a slave of Jesus the Messianic King to the Gentiles, serving as priest of God's gospel that the offering of the nations may become acceptable, having been totally dedicated in the Holy Spirit.

I have, then, a right to boast in Messianic King Jesus in the things pertaining to God. For I don't dare speak anything that Christ didn't accomplish through me to bring about the obedience of Gentiles in word and deed, in the power of signs and wonders, in the power of God's spirit; so that I, starting from Jerusalem and circling about as far as Illyricum, have fully proclaimed the Messianic King's gospel. And I consider it an honor to proclaim the gospel, not where the Messianic King was already known (so that I might not build upon another's foundation) but just as it was written, "Those who were not informed about him shall see; and those who have not heard shall understand."

Wherefore, also, I had been restrained many times from coming to you, and now the I no longer have a place in these parts and have been longing to come to you for many years, when I happen to go to Spain I will also come to you. For I hope that in going through to see you (and then be sent forward from there by you), that by seeing you first, I shall at least in part be complete.

And now I go on to Jerusalem, ministering to the saints. For Macedonia and Achaia were well pleased in extending altruism to the poor among the saints in Jerusalem. Yes they were well pleased, and they are obligated to them. For if the nations participated in their spiritual things, then they are obliged to also minister to them in the material things. Then when I have finished and have acknowledged to them this productive result, I will return through you, to Spain. And I'm sure that my coming to you has the fullest blessing of the Messianic King.

And I call upon you, brothers, through our master Jesus the Messianic King, and through the spirit's love, to contend together with me in the prayers for me unto God, that I might be rescued from those who are disobedient in Judea and that my mediation in Jerusalem may be acceptable to the saints; so that I may come joyfully to you in God's will and recuperate in your company.

Now the God of peace be with you all. Amen.

Chapter 31
The Greeting

As mentioned previously, the beginning greeting in Hellenistic letters is formulaically cheerful. But that doesn't mean that Paul didn't make creative use out of the greeting. On the contrary, Paul knew that he was going to be addressing a lack of faithfulness to the neighbor-based commands with all four groups: the Hypocrites, the Judaizers, the Mental, and the Predestined Proud. So he creatively wove in 'terms of obedience' at every possible turn in his construction of the greeting:

Romans 1:1 - 14

Paul, a **bondservant** of Jesus **the Messianic King**, called to be an apostle, appointed for the good news of God which he previously promised through his prophets in sacred scriptures concerning his son (the descendant of David according to the flesh, the one declared the son of God in power out of resurrecting from the dead according to the spirit of consecration) Jesus **the Messianic King our master**; through whom we received favor and apostleship into **faith's obedience** among all the nations on behalf of his name. Among whom are you also Jesus **the Messianic King's** invited ones. To everyone in Rome, beloved of God, the invited **loyal followers**, favor to you and peace, from God our father and Jesus **the Messianic King our master**.

First, indeed, I thank my God through Jesus **the Messianic King** because of all of you, that your faith is proclaimed in the entire world. For God is my witness, whom I serve in my spirit in the good news of his son, how constantly I mention you in my prayers, pleading (that by any means possible) that somehow I shall succeed in God's will to come to you. For I ache to see you, that somehow I might impart a spiritual favor to you for your support. That is that we might encourage each other among you out of each other's faith—both yours and mine. And I do not want you to be unaware, brothers, how often I intended to come to you (but was restrained from doing so until now) that I might obtain some fruit among you also—just like the rest of the nations. For I am obligated both to Greeks and barbarians, both to the wise and the unthinking.

The Greek term *Christos* is often translated as 'Christ' in many modern Bibles. Although this is technically correct, the full meaning of the word gets lost on the modern reader. Most people think of 'Lord Jesus Christ' as being akin to 'Sir Elton John' ('Lord' being Jesus' official title and 'Christ' being his surname). But Jesus wasn't the son of Mr. and Mrs. Christ. *Christos* was the Koine Greek equivalent of the ancient Hebrew word *Messiah*. It was a term that acknowledged Jesus as being the prophesied King (and his followers as being loyal subjects under the rule of his authority). I therefore render it 'Messianic King' to express this Hebraic word's original meaning. This helps to remind us that, each time Paul used the term, he was acknowledging Jesus as being the ruler of the Christian kingdom.

The same goes for the term 'Lord.' This term wasn't an official title the way 'Sir' is used in England today. Rather, the term meant 'Master.' It referred to someone who had total say over another's life. Hence, I render the word as 'master', as a reminder that each time Paul used the term, he was emphasizing Jesus as being the ruler of their lives.

The same goes for 'bondservant.' The Koine Greek word referred to 'being a slave,' not merely serving someone, say 'in the capacity of a waiter.' Hence, I often render the noun as 'bondservant' (or 'slave') and the verb form of this word as 'slavishly serve' ('serve as slaves'), as a reminder of the type of service being referenced.

So Paul wove in the terms 'Messianic King,' 'master,' and 'bondservant' in order to establish the king/subject and master/slave relationship between Jesus and his followers. He brilliantly worked in "faith's obedience" into his greeting as well.

The Koine Greek word *pistis* encompassed many meanings: such as faith, pledge, and faithfulness. Since Paul was later going to call all four groups into faithfulness, he made sure to let his readers know that the type of faith (the type of *pistis*) he was preaching included the aspect of faithfulness (obedience). The type of faith (*pistis*) that Paul preached was not merely 'believing something' or 'having faith in an idea.' Paul ingeniously forewarned his readers that he would be speaking of a faith that required a lifelong commitment.

To emphasize the faith/obedience link, Paul reminds his readers that they are called to be totally dedicated to God (through his use of the Koine word *hagios*). *Hagios* is often exclusively translated as 'holy' in many modern translations. While the word certainly embodies holiness, it often connoted a very important nuance, as well. It often connoted: 'total consecration to God,' 'total dedication to God.' By reminding his readers that they were called to be totally dedicated to God, he was again using the greeting to establish the theme of faithfulness, faithfulness, faithfulness.

So yes, Paul adhered to the formulaic greeting, but he did so artfully and creatively. He used the greeting to set the reader up for the message contained in the body of the letter: be faithful … or else.

Chapter 32
The Second Letter

Now we come to what is officially chapter sixteen of most Bibles' translation of Romans. The Koine papyri have allowed archaeologists to recognize that this is actually a totally complete (and separate) letter. Whether the letter was originally sent along with the first one, or later became attached, no one knows. However, it is authentically from Paul's amanuensis[172] Tertius, and therefore, appropriately belongs in the Biblical canon.

> **Romans 16:1-27**
>
> And I recommend Phebe, our sister, to you (who is an agent of the church in Cenchrea) that you receive her in the Master in a manner worthy of the saints, and assist her in whatever matter she needs your assistance, for she has been a benefactor of many, including myself.
>
> > Greet Priscilla and Aquilas, my fellow-workers in Christ Jesus who risked their own lives for mine, to whom I not only give thanks, but also to all the Gentile churches and the church at their house.
> > Greet Epaenetus, my beloved, who is Asia's first believer in the Messianic King.
> > Greet Mary, who labored so hard for us.

172 An amanuensis was a person who wrote letters for another. They would write down the dictation.

> Greet Andronicus and Junias, my kinsmen, and my fellow prisoners, who are prominent among the apostles, who also were in Messianic King before me.
> Greet Amplias, my beloved in the Master.
> Greet Arbanus, our fellow-worker in the Messianic King, and my beloved Stachys.
> Greet Apelles, the 'tried and true' in Messianic King.
> Greet those who belong to the household of Aristobulus.
> Greet Herodion, my kinsman.
> Greet those who belong to the household of Narcissus, who are in the Master.
> Greet Tryphaena, and Tryphosa, who are working in the Master.
> Greet Persis, the beloved, who labored so hard in the Master.
> Greet Rufus, the distinguished one in the Master, and his mother and mine.
> Greet Asyncritus, Phlegon, Hermas, Patrobas, Hermes, and the brothers with them.
> Greet Philologus, and Julias, Nereus, and his sister, and Olympas, and all the saints with them.
> Greet one another with a holy kiss. The churches of the Messianic King do salute you.

And I call upon you to help me, brothers, to pay careful attention to factious opposition and those who manufacture enticements that are contrary to the teaching that you learned. Turn away from them. For they don't serve our master Jesus the Messianic King. Rather they serve their own appetites. And through their eloquence and flattery they lead astray the hearts of the unsuspecting.

For your compliance has spread to all. I rejoice, therefore, in regards to you. And I want you to be wise to what is benevolent, and innocent to what is malicious. And the God of the peace shall speedily crush the Adversary under your feet; the favor of our master Jesus the Messianic King be with you. Amen.

> Greetings from Timotheus, my fellow worker, and Lucius, and Jason, and Sosipater, my kinsmen.

> I, Tertius, who wrote this letter, send greetings to you in the Lord;
> Gaius, my host, sends greetings to you and all the members of the church.
> Erastus, the steward of the city, and Quartus the brother, send their greetings to you.
>
> The favor of our master Jesus the Messianic King be with you all. Amen. And to him who is able to establish you in accordance to my gospel and **the preaching of Jesus the Messianic King, according to the disclosure of the secret which was kept silent for long ages past, and now has been revealed, also, through the scriptures of the Prophets, according to a command from the God of the ages, has now been made known to all the nations unto faith's obedience.**
>
> To the only wise God, through Jesus the Messianic King, to him be majesty through the ages. Amen.

Did you notice how even this short letter begins with a greetings section, moves immediately into the body, then immediately transitions to salutations? Do you recall that Paul's longer letter (which preceded this one) included all those elements as well? This is how archaeologists recognized that what is officially referred to as chapter sixteen of Romans is, in actuality, a separate and complete letter in and of itself.

While there's so little meat in this short letter, what incredible meat there is! Jesus disclosed a secret that has been kept silent for long ages past … a secret that was already revealed through the prophets, a secret which accords with a command from the God of the ages. Obedient faith to this secret is what Paul calls "faith's obedience."

So what did Jesus preach that was already disclosed by the Prophets, which accords with a command from God? "Treat others the same way you want to be treated for this is the Law and the Prophets." Jesus said that the Prophet Hosea taught this, but the Jews haven't heeded it since (it was kept silent). Jesus said that the entire Law is fulfilled through one command from the God of the ages: "Love your neighbor as yourself." It was Jesus' Sermon on the Mount where he disclosed the secret that has been kept silent for long ages past, a secret revealed by the prophets that accords with a command from God. This secret, now disclosed, is the foundation of Paul's second letter … and his first as well.

Chapter 33
Putting It All Together

There we have it. We have uncovered the structure of Romans from beginning to end. We have reconciled the entire letter with Jesus' teachings in Matthew. The Granddaddy of Biblical puzzles is solved.

Greetings	(1:1—1:16)
The Body	
The Hypocrites	(1:17—2:16)
The Judaizers	(2:17—5:21)
The Mental	(6:1—8:27)
The Predestined Proud	(8:28—11:36)
The Ending	
Conclusion	(12:1—15:7)
Salutations	(15:8—15:33)
The Second Letter	(16:1—16:26)

Should you ever get confused and wonder why Paul is saying what he's saying, just find out where you are in the letter's structure and his reasoning should become quite clear to you.

So now that we've solved the *structure* of Romans, can we use it to find the *key*? Let's summarize every section containing theology:

- *Hypocrites*—Don't think you are going to escape the equitable judgment of God, who will judge everyone by the benevolence of their deeds.

- *Judaizers*—Only the followers of the Justices of the Law will be vindicated before God. By the Jobs of the Law, no flesh will be vindicated in his sight.

- *Mental*—If you do not fulfill the Law's requirement of Justice through the spirit, then you are going to die.

- *Predestined Proud*—If you stop treating other people kindly, then you will be cut off.

- *Second Letter*—Jesus preached a secret which no one spoke about, even though it was revealed by the prophets and accords with a command from God.

So, what then is the key? What is the one statement that encompasses them all? Well, let's think about this for a moment. Paul was a Christian. Paul believed in Jesus. Wouldn't Paul teach the same thing that his master taught him?

We saw in the previous sections that Jesus taught: I have not come to abolish the Law and the Prophets because only the neighbor-based commands are the Law and the Prophets. Every first century Jew understood exactly what Jesus meant: *Only the neighbor-based commands count; the Jobs of the Law count for nothing.* Paul was a first century Jew. So he knew what Jesus meant:

- **Only the neighbor-based commands count; the Jobs of the Law count for nothing.** Therefore, don't think you are going to escape the equitable judgment of God, who will judge everyone by the benevolence of their deeds.

- **Only the neighbor-based commands count; the Jobs of the Law count for nothing.** Therefore, only the followers of the Justices of the Law will be vindicated before God. By the Jobs of the Law, no flesh will be vindicated in his sight.

- **Only the neighbor-based commands count; the Jobs of the Law count for nothing.** Therefore, if you do not fulfill the Law's requirement of Justice through the spirit, you are going to die.

- **Only the neighbor-based commands count; the Jobs of the Law count for nothing.** Therefore, if you stop treating other people kindly, then you will be cut off.

- **Only the neighbor-based commands count; the Jobs of the Law count for nothing.** Therefore, Jesus preached this secret that no one spoke about, even though it was revealed by the prophets and accords with a command from God.

Should we be surprised that Paul taught the same thing Jesus did? Of course not! But the startling reality is that no one could reconcile Paul's letter to the Romans with Jesus *because the Christian faith didn't know what Jesus taught for fifteen hundred years*. However, recent research into first century Jewish culture and Law has finally given us enough inputs to know what Jesus taught in the highly Hebraic Gospels. In fact, this is the first generation in fifteen hundred years to have enough tools to unravel all the New Testament books. And now, because of this, the Romans code has finally been broken.

Chapter 34
Paul's Bible

So what about Romans 1:17, the verse that started the Protestant Reformation in the first place? Given the historical importance of this verse, it deserves a chapter all of its own.

Modern Bibles are trying to slowly ease Christians into recognizing a very disturbing fact: The Christian Bible has been using the wrong version of the Old Testament for fifteen hundred years. For example, if you look up Romans 2:24 in the NIV Bible, you will find the following:

> As it is written: "God's name is blasphemed among the Gentiles because of you."

And if you check the NIV's footnote for Romans 2:24, you will see the following:

> Isaiah 52:5 (see Septuagint)

The footnote informs the reader that Paul is quoting the Septuagint version of Isaiah 52:5.

So what, then, is this Septuagint? And why does today's bestselling Christian Bible refer its readers to it? The answer is both short and profound: The NIV is trying to gently tell its readers that Paul quoted a different version of the Old Testament than the one found in the NIV itself. If you look up Isaiah 52:5 in the NIV, you will find:

> And all day long my name is constantly blasphemed.

Where is the phrase "because of you" and where are "the Gentiles?" After all, these items are crucial to what Paul said "is written." However, they certainly are not written in the NIV's Old Testament, or in any other populist Bible, for that matter. These phrases were written in a different version of the Old Testament—a version called the Septuagint (also known as the LXX). The Septuagint version of Isaiah 52:5 says:

> And because of you my name is always blasphemed among the Gentiles.[173]

This is why the NIV had to let its readers know that Paul quoted a different version of the Old Testament than the one used in modern Bibles. But the answer is the problem: *Paul quoted a version of the Old Testament that is different from the one used in modern Bibles.*[174] To see more examples, take a look at the NIV's footnotes for Romans 3:14, Romans 9:28, Romans 10:11, Romans 11:27, Romans 15:12 and Romans 15:21.

When Christians realize their Bibles contain a different version of the Old Testament than the one Paul quoted, it's natural for them to become unnerved. Populist theologians do their best to assure their followers that the differences between modern Old Testaments and the Septuagint are negligible. But is this really true? The differences between the two versions certainly played a pivotal role in the life of Martin Luther—the "father of the Protestant Reformation."

But to understand the history-changing event caused by a mix-up of the different Old Testament versions, we must first discuss the concept of words having multiple meanings.

All languages contain words that have multiple meanings. Consider the following examples:

- The English word *pool* can refer to 'a body of water' or 'billiards.'

173 Isaiah 52:5 LXX

174 *The Jerome Conspiracy* by Michael Wood documents the history of how and why the original version of the Old Testament was replaced with a different one.

- The English word *port* can refer to 'a type of wine' or 'the left side of a ship.'

- The English word *bank* can refer to 'a financial institution' or 'the slope of a hill.'

- And so on, and so on.

Like all languages, Koine Greek also contained words that had multiple meanings. For example, the Koine word *pistis* could refer to 'faith' or 'faithfulness.' *Pistis* could refer to 'believing in something' or to 'having fidelity to someone.'

So how does a person know when *pistis* referred to 'faith' or 'faithfulness?' Most of the time, it's very easy. Just like English, the topic of conversation almost always narrows the meaning down to one choice. For example:

He was playing *pool.*	(The topic shows us that *pool* means 'billiards.')
He drank *port.*	(The topic shows us that *port* means 'a type of wine.')
He withdrew money from the *bank.*	(The topic shows us that *bank* means 'a financial institution.')

Very often the topic makes the meaning so clear that we don't even think about all the possible meanings of the words as we read the sentences. We just naturally think of the one meaning that fits the topic.

With this in mind, let's explore the Koine word *pistis* by going back to the first century and placing ourselves into the shoes of the original readers of the following passage:

> You need to persevere in order to obtain the promise from doing the will of God:
>
>> For in a little while the coming one will arrive without delay. And the just man shall live out of *pistis* and my soul will be displeased if he shrinks back.
>
> But we are not those who shrink back to destruction, but *pistis* to the preserving of the soul.

The topic of the passage lets us know the meaning of *pistis*. In fact, the topic points to one meaning three times over:

Topic:	You need to persevere to obtain the promise.
Meaning:	Faithfulness
Topic:	If he shrinks back God's soul will be displeased.
Meaning:	Faithfulness
Topic:	We are not those who shrink back to destruction.
Meaning:	Faithfulness

The passage consistently and congruently calls for *faithfulness*. It doesn't even call for ordinary faithfulness, but lifelong faithfulness to the preserving of the soul. The passage is faithfulness on steroids. Any first century Koine Greek reader would have instantly understood the passage as follows:

> You need to persevere in order to obtain the promise from doing the will of God:
>
>> For in a little while the coming one will arrive without delay. But the just man shall live out of **faithfulness,** and so if he shrinks back my soul will be displeased with him.
>
> But we are not those who shrink back to destruction, but **faithfulness** to the preserving of the soul.

This passage is found in the Biblical book of Hebrews.[175] Thanks to the author of Hebrews, we have documentation on how the first century Christians interpreted the following passage from the Septuagint (the original Old Testament):

> For in a little while the coming one will arrive without delay. But the just man shall live out of **faithfulness,** and so if he shrinks back my soul will have no pleasure in him.[176]

The author of Hebrews informs us of two important things:

- First, it shows us how Habakkuk 2:3-4 read in the first century Septuagint.
- Second, it documents the first century Christian interpretation of Habakkuk 2:3-4: This passage means "you need to persevere to obtain the promise" for "those who shrink back destroy their souls." The first century Christians understood Habakkuk 2:3-4 as containing both a strong promise and a strong warning regarding the need for lifelong faithfulness.

With this in mind, let's consider Paul's issues with the Roman Christians. All four groups (the Hypocrites, the Judaizers, the Mental, and the Predestined Proud) were flirting with the unjust treatment of others. So, immediately after Paul wrote the requisite greeting, he began the body of his letter with Habakkuk's dual promise and warning: the promise that they will live because of faithfulness and the warning that shrinking back will destroy their souls:

> For in the gospel God's justice is brought to light out of *pistis* into *pistis*, **just as it is written, "The just man shall live out his *pistis*." For the wrath of God is brought to light from heaven upon all the impiety and injustice of men, who hinder the truth in injustice**[177]

Paul used Habakkuk 2:4 to warn the Roman Christians that if they treated others unjustly, then **they would assuredly suffer God's**

175 Quite oddly populist Bibles still translate *pistis* as 'faith' in the Hebrews' passage. They ignore the topic. They try to squeeze the square peg of 'faith' into the round holes of 'only reaping the reward through perseverance' and 'not shrinking back to the destruction of the soul'.

176 Habakkuk 2:4 LXX

177 Romans 1:17-18

wrath for "hindering the truth in injustice." In other words, Paul quoted Habakkuk 2:4 to remind the Romans that they will destroy their souls if they shrink back—if they return to a life of selfishness and injustice. (Paul used Habakkuk 2:4 in the exact same way that the author of Hebrews did.)

So it all seems pretty cut and dry, doesn't it? It would have remained cut and dry if it wasn't for the day when the Septuagint—the Old Testament version quoted by Jesus and his apostles—was thrown into the trash. Everything changed when the Christian Bible began using a new version of the Old Testament. When the church changed Old Testament versions, they changed the versions of every Old Testament book, including Habakkuk. And the new version of Habakkuk discusses a completely different topic in Habakkuk 2:3-4:

> Though the message tarries, wait for it. For it will certainly come. It will not delay. Behold, as for the proud man, his soul isn't right within him. But the just man will live by his faith.

Where the Septuagint (the original Christian Old Testament) discussed the coming *Messianic King*, the new Old Testament discusses a coming visionary *message*. Where the original Old Testament *included a warning about shrinking back*, the new Old Testament *doesn't even have this warning*. In other words, the original Old Testament's message about 'not shrinking back from faithfulness to the coming Messiah' was replaced with 'having faith in a coming message.' It was only a matter of time before this significant change blew up in the world's face.

It cannot be stressed enough that when the topic of Habakkuk 2:4 changed, so did the meaning of *pistis*. It had to. Allow me to illustrate:

Original Topic:	He was playing *pool*.
New Topic:	He was swimming in the *pool*.
Result:	The meaning of *pool* changes from 'billiards' to 'body of water.'

* * *

Original Topic:	He withdrew some money from the *bank.*
New Topic:	He sat down on the *bank.*
Result:	The meaning of *bank* changes from 'a financial institution' to 'the slope of a hill.'

* * *

Original Topic:	He drank the *port.*
New Topic:	The sailor stood on the *port.*
Result:	The meaning of *port* changes from 'a type of wine' to 'the left side of a ship.'

When the topic changes, then the meanings of words change as well. This is precisely what happened to *pistis* in Paul's quote of Habakkuk 2:4. When the topic changed, then the meaning of the word changed:

Original Topic:	Those who don't shrink back shall live because of their *pistis.*
New Topic:	Those who trust the message shall live because of their *pistis.*
Result:	The meaning of *pistis* changed from 'faithfulness' to 'faith.'

Paul originally quoted Habakkuk 2:4 to remind the Romans that they need lifelong faithfulness to the Messiah's teaching … or else they will destroy their souls. But when Paul's version of the Jewish scriptures was tossed into the trash, his version of Habakkuk 2:4 was trashed as well. The new Old Testament brought with it a new version of Habakkuk 2:4. **Lifelong faithfulness to the Messiah was trashed, and faith in a message became the new game in town.**

Now let's fast forward to the beginning of the Protestant Reformation. Sometime around 1517 CE, a German Monk named Martin Luther read Paul's quote of Habakkuk 2:4 and it changed his life forever. **Martin Luther wrote, on many occasions, that it was Paul's quote of Habakkuk 2:4 that resulted in his epiphany that**

salvation comes from faith in the message of the gospel.[178]

That's right! Martin Luther didn't know that Paul's quote was written at a time when Habakkuk 2:4 discussed *lifelong faithfulness to the Messiah*. Martin Luther assumed Paul's Bible was the same as his. Therefore, he wrongly concluded that Paul was writing about *faith in a message*. Based on this misunderstanding, Martin Luther lit the torch of 'salvation of all sins by faith alone.'

The swapping of the Old Testaments eventually resulted in Martin Luther believing that he had discovered a truth that his monastic teachers were ignoring. Unfortunately, he was a rebel without a real cause, but the fake cause caught on anyway. And the rest, as they say, is history.

178 From "Martin Luther's Tower Experience," article by Dr. Richard P. Bucher

Chapter 35
The Results Are In

The purpose of Biblical Cryptanalysis is to elevate biblical discovery above subjective debate and theologizing. Seamless continuity is empirical proof that a discourse's message has truly been recovered. And Biblical Cryptanalysis offers two methods for objectively determining when seamless continuity has been finally achieved: identification of the *structure* from beginning to end and/or identification of the *key* (the single statement that accounts for every sentence from beginning to end). Once the seamless structure and/or key have been identified, we know we are done. We know, with total certainty, we have successfully recovered the overarching message of the discourse (or set of teachings) under analysis.

And, at least for the most important passages in the entire Bible, the results are in. The structures have been assembled and the keys have been identified. Seven of the most important biblical puzzles are finally solved once for all.

Puzzle 1

The first teaching in the body of the Sermon on the Mount: *Unless you treat people better than the scribes and the Pharisees you cannot enter the Kingdom of Heaven.*

- You have heard 'don't murder' and 'those who murder shall be liable to the court.'
    - **But I tell you that you have to treat people better than that.** Anyone who is angry with his brother is liable to the court and anyone who calls his brother a name is in danger of hellfire.
- You have heard 'don't commit adultery.'
    - **But I tell you that you have to treat people better than that.** Don't ogle a woman lustfully with your eyes or you're already an adulterer. It would be better for you to have no eyes if you can't stop offending your wife and the woman you are ogling.
- It was said that anyone can divorce his wife simply by giving her a certificate of divorce.
    - **But I tell you that you have to treat people better than that.** You can only divorce a woman if she's been unfaithful to you. And anyone who marries the divorced unfaithful woman shares in her adultery.
- You have heard the ancients were told not to make false vows, but to fulfill vows to the Lord.
    - **But I tell you that you have to treat people better than that.** Just keep your word even without oaths. Let your 'yes' be 'yes' and your 'no' be 'no'. Period.
- You have heard 'an eye for an eye, and a tooth for a tooth.'
    - **But I tell you that you have to treat people better than that.** Don't take revenge on a person who injures you. Offer him assistance instead.
- You have heard that you should love your countrymen and hate your enemies.
    - **But I tell you that you have to treat people better than that.** You need to love your enemies and pray for those who harm you. Otherwise you will not reap the reward.

Puzzle 2

The full body of the Sermon on the Mount: *God is going to treat you based on how you treat others.*

1. **God is going to treat you based on how you treat others.** Therefore, only if you treat people better than the scribes and the Pharisees can you enter the kingdom of heaven. (Matthew 5:20-48)
2. **God is going to treat you based on how you treat others.** Therefore, your father in heaven will reward you when you secretly give to the poor. (Matthew 6:1-4)
3. **God is going to treat you based on how you treat others.** Therefore, God will forgive your sins in direct proportion to your forgiveness of others. (Matthew 6:5-15)
4. **God is going to treat you based on how you treat others.** Therefore, you store up treasures in heaven by generously sharing with those in need. (Matthew 6:19-24)
5. **God is going to treat you based on how you treat others.** Therefore, don't worry about your own needs. Just focus on bringing God's kingdom to earth by expressing loving kindness, and God will meet your needs as well. (Matthew 6:25-34)
6. **God is going to treat you based on how you treat others.** Therefore, whatever measure you use on others God will use on you. (Matthew 7:1-6)
7. **God is going to treat you based on how you treat others.** Therefore, treat others well, because as a child of God your heavenly Father will give you far greater rewards than you can possibly give even to your own family. (Matthew 7:7-11)

Puzzle 3

The warnings at the end of the Sermon on the Mount: *Only those who actually follow Jesus' interpretation of the Law will make it on judgment day.*

- Treat others the same way you want to be treated for this is the Law.
    - **Only those who actually follow this interpretation of the Law will make it on judgment day.** For the low quality trees bearing worthless fruit will be chopped up and thrown into the fire.
    - **Only those who actually follow this interpretation of the Law will make it on judgment day.** For I will say, "Get away from me you who broke the Law."
    - **Only those who actually follow this interpretation of the Law will make it on judgment day.** For everyone who hears these words of mine and ignores them will be destroyed like a house built on sand during a storm.

Puzzle 4

The structure of the Sermon on the Mount

I. **Beatitudes**: Jesus calls the crowds to gather around him.

II. **Introduction**: Jesus announces he has come to give an interpretation of the Law and the Prophets that encompasses every commandment down to the smallest one.

III. **Body**: God is going to treat you based solely on how you treat others.

   a. *Only if you treat people better than the scribes and the Pharisees can you enter the kingdom of heaven.*

   b. *Your Father in heaven will reward you when you secretly give to the poor.*

   c. *God will forgive your sins in direct proportion to your forgiveness of others.*

   d. *You store up treasures in heaven by generously sharing with those in need.*

   e. *Don't worry about your own needs. Just focus on bringing God's kingdom to earth by expressing loving kindness, and God will meet your needs as well.*

   f. *Whatever measure you use on others God will use on you.*

   g. *Treat others well, because as a child of God your heavenly Father will give you far greater rewards than you can possibly give even to your own family.*

IV. **Conclusion**: In everything, therefore, treat others the same way you want to be treated for this is the Law and the Prophets; the narrow road to life. [This is the interpretation that encompasses all the commandments of scripture down to the smallest one.]

V. **Warnings**: Only those who actually follow this interpretation of the Law will make it on judgment day.

   a. *The low quality trees bearing worthless fruit will be chopped up and thrown into the fire.*

   b. *I will say, "Get away from me you who broke the Law."*

   c. *Everyone who hears these words of mine and ignores them will be destroyed like a house built on sand during a storm.*

Puzzle 5

The key to all of Jesus' teachings on salvation and judgment in the Gospel of Matthew (including the very key to the Sermon on the Mount): *Jesus didn't come to abolish the Law and the Prophets because only the neighbor-based commands are the Law and the Prophets.*

- **I have not come to abolish the Law and the Prophets because only the neighbor-based commands are the Law and the Prophets.** Therefore, treating others the same way you want to be treated is the Law and the Prophets.

- **I have not come to abolish the Law and the Prophets because only the neighbor-based commands are the Law and the Prophets.** Therefore, people will inherit the kingdom because of their acts of loving kindness.

- **I have not come to abolish the Law and the Prophets because only the neighbor-based commands are the Law and the Prophets.** Therefore, God desires loving kindness shown to others, not animal sacrifice, for the forgiveness of sins.

- **I have not come to abolish the Law and the Prophets because only the neighbor-based commands are the Law and the Prophets.** Therefore, if you want to inherit life in the coming age, follow all the commandments based on loving your neighbor as yourself.

- **I have not come to abolish the Law and the Prophets because only the neighbor-based commands are the Law and the Prophets.** Therefore, by fulfilling the command to love your neighbor as yourself, you are fulfilling the command to love God with your whole being.

Puzzle 6

The structure of Paul's letter(s) to the Romans:

Greetings	(1:1—1:16)
The Body	
The Hypocrites	(1:17—2:16)
The Judaizers	(2:17—5:21)
The Mental	(6:1—8:27)
The Predestined Proud	(8:28—11:36)
The Ending	
Conclusion	(12:1—15:7)
Salutations	(15:8—15:33)
The Second Letter	(16:1—16:26)

Puzzle 7

The key to Paul's letter(s) to the Romans: *Only the neighbor based commands count, the Jobs of the Law count for nothing.*

- **Only the neighbor-based commands count; the Jobs of the Law count for nothing.** Therefore, don't think you are going to escape the equitable judgment of God who will judge everyone by the benevolence of their deeds. (*The Hypocrites*)
- **Only the neighbor-based commands count; the Jobs of the Law count for nothing.** Therefore, only the followers of the Justices of the Law will be vindicated before God. By the Jobs of the Law, no flesh will be vindicated in his sight. (*The Judaizers*)
- **Only the neighbor-based commands count; the Jobs of the Law count for nothing.** Therefore, if you do not fulfill the Law's requirement of Justice through the spirit you are going to die. (*The Mental*)
- **Only the neighbor-based commands count; the Jobs of the Law count for nothing.** Therefore, if you stop treating other people kindly, then you will be cut off. (*The Predestined Proud*)
- **Only the neighbor-based commands count; the Jobs of the Law count for nothing.** Therefore, Jesus preached this secret that no one spoke about even though it was revealed by the prophets and accords with a command from God. (*The Second Letter*)

It's time to stop treating the teachings of Jesus and Paul as if they are debatable. The moment we view them from the perspective of their first century audience, we know with total certainty the message they both delivered. The puzzles are solved and the codes are broken. The results are in.

Chapter 36
Retro Christianity

Thanks to Biblical Cryptanalysis we finally know the original message that launched Christianity in the first place. Both Jesus and the religious leaders taught that the Jewish Law will remain intact forever. However the religious leaders taught an interpretation of the Law consisting of two distinct subsets: commandments between man and God, commandments between man and neighbor. Whereas Jesus taught that only the neighbor based commands are the Law.

The original Christian faith is unique among all religions. Christianity wasn't just another religion that contained the Golden Rule; rather, Christianity *was* the Golden Rule. And that made all the difference.

The human mind cannot focus on two things at once (let alone three, four ... six hundred thirteen things). Focus, by definition, requires attention being placed on one thing, and one thing *only*. Jesus knew that. He knew that people wouldn't start truly taking care of each other unless they realized that it's the *only* thing that matters.

The *Epistle of Barnabas*, the *Didache*, and other early Christian writings inform us of the doctrinal purity of the original faith. This period of doctrinal purity is punctuated by a most remarkable degree of humanitarianism ... perhaps an unparalleled degree at that. Consider this letter written to the first century Corinthian Church:

> We know that many among us gave themselves up unto bonds, that they might deliver others. Many have given themselves up unto slavery, and, having received their own price, have therewith fed others.[179]

Many Corinthians gave themselves over to lifelong bondage solely to free others from the same horrible plight. *Many* Corinthians offered themselves into slavery just to use their purchase price to buy food for others. It is one thing to die for others. It's another to offer the rest of your life in servitude solely for the sake of meeting the humanitarian needs of others. And this was happening *en masse.*

Don't think for a moment that I'm cherry picking. An entire volume could be written about the historic self-sacrificial deeds of the early Christians. The original Christians, for a couple *centuries,* displayed a level of love possibly unlike any the world had ever seen before … and has ever seen since.

The Orthodoxy that took over by the fifth century was established by non-Jewish individuals. Their non-Jewish heritage didn't make them bad people, but it did make them highly uninformed about the actual meaning of the Hebraic Biblical text. When Orthodoxy took over, the seemingly fragmented nature of the Biblical text resulted in the piling of one doctrine on top of another. The doctrinal distractions of Orthodoxy achieved for the Christians the same result that the Jobs of the Law achieved for the Jews. Pretty soon, the non-Golden Rule doctrines were *the* reason for the faith; so much so that people were even willing to kill for them.

By the time the Protestant Reformation began, knowledge regarding the differences between Classical and Koine Greek was nonexistent. That, coupled with a scant understanding of first century Jewish culture and Law, caused the faith to step further away from its roots, rather than reclaim them.

The twentieth century will forever be considered a most remarkable time for Biblical archaeology. It brought with it the Koine Greek language and a plethora of knowledge regarding first century Jewish culture and Law. For the first time in over fifteen hundred years, the world finally has sufficient inputs to decode the original teachings

179 1 Clement 55:2 as translated by Charles H. Hoole

of the Christian text.

It wasn't my initial intention to find a single key that accounts for all the New Testament teachings on salvation and judgment. I had only set out to apply my cryptanalytic skills to the cave four Dead Sea Scrolls. I wanted to find the reason why these scrolls were suppressed for thirty years after they were discovered. I instinctively knew that there was a juicy real-world mystery lurking behind the event. But I certainly didn't expect it to lead to the realization of a new understanding of the teachings of Jesus, and the radical message that birthed the Christian faith.

Yet, because of the uniqueness of Christianity (the fact that it was founded on a single principle), cryptanalysis turned out to be a most effective approach for decoding the New Testament books. No other religion (because of the plethora of requirements) would have lent itself to such an approach. But, because of Christianity's uniqueness, what began as cryptanalysis of cave four documents ended up solving the key to the original Christian faith.

A puzzle that no one knew even existed inadvertently ended up getting solved. We now know the full meaning of Jesus' most important sermon. When Jesus of Nazareth ascended the Mount of Olives, he discarded one subset of the Jewish Law while leaving the other subset fully intact. Jesus discarded the Works of the Law while leaving the neighbor-based commands fully intact.

When archaeologists discovered a first century scroll entitled "Some Works of the Law" in cave four, it must've sent a chill through Orthodox leaders. It is little wonder why the contents of cave four were suppressed for so long, for the scroll was the key to unlocking a two-thousand-year-old mystery—the lost doctrinal basis of the original Christian faith. But now, thanks to archaeology, cryptography, and a good bit of luck, the original message that Jesus delivered on the Mount of Olives has been rediscovered once again. And we have found, within this sermon, the key to breaking the Romans code.

For centuries, Paul's misunderstood letter to the Romans distracted Christians away from a childlike acceptance of the Golden

Rule as the only path to God. Yet we have found that Paul himself preached this very ideal to his Roman converts after all. Not only that, Paul taught that, aside from a blessed few, everyone needs the spirit of Jesus to live up to that ideal. This is the reason Jesus came. This is the way in which Jesus ultimately saves people from their sins—by empowering them to abandon their selfish existence and truly love their fellowman as much as they love their very selves.

For fifteen hundred years, Christians didn't know "the Works of the Law" referred to the *mitzvot bein adam lamakom* (commands between man and God). Thus, in turn, they didn't recognize "the Justices of the Law" as a reference to the *mitzvot bein adam lachaveiro* (commands between man and his neighbor). So, for fifteen hundred years, Christians didn't know Romans taught about the neighbor-based commands which vindicate and the Works of the Law which do not.

But now, two millenia after Paul's letter was originally written, the precise constitution of the Works of the Law has been fully recovered. The Romans Code has been broken.

Appendix A
Prove It

It's time to finally address the good, the bad, the ugly—the proven, the disproven, and the indeterminate. Mathematics has developed a method for testing whether a proposed idea is proven 100%, disproven 100%, or indeterminate (neither proven or disproven, still in need of more inputs).

Let me give you a simple example. Consider the following two inputs:

P = Tom ate an almond.

Q = Almonds contain zinc.

Based on these inputs, can you classify the following three propositions?

Proposition 1: Tom didn't eat zinc.

Proposition 2: Tom did eat zinc.

Proposition 3: Tom ate sulfur.

The convergence of P and Q tells us that "Tom ate an almond containing zinc." Based on this convergence, we can classify the propositions as follows:

Proposition 1: Tom didn't eat zinc.	**Disproven**
Proposition 2: Tom did eat zinc.	**Proven**
Proposition 3: Tom ate sulfur.	**Indeterminate**

If P and Q are true then we can say, with absolute certainty—beyond debate—beyond refutation that "Tom did eat zinc." You can debate P. You can reject Q. But if you accept P and Q then you must accept the logical extension of them: Tom ate some zinc. This is the beauty of propositional logic.

Equally beautiful is the ability to disprove propositions. If P and Q are true, then the proposed idea that Tom didn't eat zinc is proven false. No 'ifs,' 'ands,' or 'buts' about it. It is disproven 100%.

With this in mind, let's look at three propositions regarding the teachings of Jesus and Paul:

Orthodox Catholicism: Jesus abolished the Jewish Law and established one of his own, one that involves two kinds of commands (commands between man and God, commands between man and neighbor). The commandments between man and neighbor are not sufficient for salvation. One must follow Jesus' Law, belong to the Catholic Church, and keep the sacraments.

Orthodox Protestantism: Jesus abolished the entire Law. Christians are not obligated any Law whatsoever. Salvation is a free gift from God received by faith.

MW: Jesus did not come to abolish the Law because only the neighbor based commandments are the Law.

So which of these propositions is: proven, disproven, or indeterminate? Before we dive in, allow me to explain some very simple mathematical notation. Consider the following variable:

A = Treating others the same way you want to be treated is the entire Law.

Mathematicians use the ~ symbol to represent the negation of a variable. For example:

~A = Treating others the same way you want to be treated is not the entire Law.

Simple, right? So let's take a look at some Biblical variables.

A = Treating others the same way you want to be treated is the entire Law.—Matthew 7:12, Jesus

B = I have not come to abolish the Law.—Matthew 5:17, Jesus

C = Those who follow the kind of commands based on loving your neighbor as yourself inherit life in the age to come.—Matthew 19:17-19, Jesus

D = Humanity will be divided into two groups based solely on the benevolence of their deeds.—Matthew 25:31-46, Jesus

E = God desires loving kindness shown to others for the forgiveness of sins instead of animal sacrifice.—Matthew 9:13 & 12:7, Jesus

F = The Christian faith is the opposite of annulling the Law. Rather, it preserves the Law.—Romans 3:31, Paul

G = Only those who follow the Law are vindicated before God—Romans 2:13, Paul

H = Every commandment in the Law is recapitulated in the statement, "Love your neighbor as yourself."—Romans 13-8-9 & Galatians 5:14, Paul

I = Whoever bears the burdens of others has fulfilled Christ's interpretation of the Law.—Galatians 6:2, Paul

J = Unbelieving Gentiles who instinctively keep the Justices of the Law are vindicated before God for doing so.—Romans 2:13-15, 26, Paul

Now let test the three propositions:

MW	Catholicism	Protestantism
A	~A	~A
B	~B	~B
C	~C	~C
D	~D	~D
E	~E	~E
F	~F	~F
G	G	~G
H	~H	~H
I	~I	~I
J	~J	~J

What does this table mean? If A through J are true, then Orthodox Christianity is not true. This is the inescapable conclusion.

Does this table prove MW is true? No, it only shows that MW doesn't negate A through J.

So is there any way to prove MW is true based on A through J? Yes, there is. We can do this by testing the negation of MW.

MW is as follows:

> MW = Jesus did not come to abolish the Law because only the neighbor based commandments are the Law.

Therefore the negation of MW is:

> ~MW = Jesus abolished the Law and/or the neighbor-based commands are not the entire Law.

What does testing the negation of MW accomplish? If the negation of a statement is proven FALSE, then the opposite of the negation is proven TRUE. For example, if "Mary's rose is not red" is proven FALSE, then "Mary's rose is red" is proven TRUE. Likewise:

> If "Jesus abolished the Law" is proven FALSE
>
> And if "The neighbor-based commandments are not the entire Law" is proven FALSE
>
> Then "Jesus didn't abolish the Law because only the neighbor-based commandments are the Law" is **proven TRUE**.

So let's assign some variables and test ~MW.

X = Jesus abolished the Law.

Z = The neighbor based commands are not the entire Law.

X Jesus abolished the Law	Y The neighbor-based commands are not the entire Law.
~B	~A
~C	~C
~F	~D
~G	~H
~J	~I

B, C, F, G, and J all prove X is not true. A, C, D, H, and I all prove Y is not true. So, if A through J are true, then X and Y are both not true, and therefore **MW is proven to be true**.

In other words: To embrace A through J is to embrace MW, and to embrace Orthodox Christianity is to reject A through J. Love it or hate it, these are the only choices A through J afford. This is as sure at the earth revolves around the sun and $e = mc^2$. This is empirical reality.

Appendix B
The Stages of the Ages

In breaking the Romans code, we discussed how Paul told the Predestined Proud that everyone (including those they were gloating over) would be reconciled to God. This likely seems incongruous to most readers. On one hand, Paul teaches that those who are selfish and unjust are going to suffer God's wrath. On the other hand, Paul taught that everyone, including the blinded Jews, is going to be reconciled to God. How could Paul possibly consider both of these to be true?

> **For I don't want you to be ignorant, brothers, of the following secret knowledge (in order for you not to be conceited): the blindness on part of Israel has come about only until the fullness of the Gentiles enters in, and in this manner all Israel will be saved.** Just as it is written, "The rescuer shall come from out of Zion, and he shall take away the Godless deeds from Jacob. And this is the covenant to them by me, when I take away their sins."
>
> In regard to the gospel they have become detested for your sake, but in regards to the selection beloved for the sake of the fathers. **For the favors and the selection of God are not to be regretted: For just as you chosen ones once disobeyed God but now have been shown mercy because of the blinded ones' disobedience; so also the blinded ones who are now disobedient will be shown mercy because of the mercy shown to you chosen ones. For God imprisoned everyone in disobedience in order for him to show mercy to everyone.**[180]

So where did Paul get such an idea? In the Jewish scriptures,

180 Romans 11:25-32

Israel was the archetype of 'the chosen ones,' while Sodom was the archetype of 'the disobedient ones.' With this in mind, consider the following prophecy written in Ezekiel:

> Your older sister is Samaria and her daughters who dwell on your left. And your younger sister is Sodom and her daughters who dwell on your right. And you did not behave as they did, nor act even a little bit in their lawlessness, rather you have outdone them all in what you have done. As surely as I live, says Adonia the Master, has Sodom and her daughters behaved in the same manner as you and your daughters? After all, the violation of your sister Sodom was haughtiness. She and her daughters lived luxuriously; completely full of bread and prosperity. They had all of this and they didn't assist the poor and the needy. And they bragged and committed lawlessness before me, and I removed them as you saw. And Samaria didn't sin half as much as you. **And you multiplied your lawlessness above them, and vindicated your sisters in all the lawlessness you did.** And now bear the pain that you have brought upon yourself, in which you have spoiled your sisters in your sins in which your lawlessness deeds far surpassed theirs, and vindicated them above yourself. **Now be ashamed and bear your disgrace in vindicating your sisters. And I will turn back their rejection (the rejection of Sodom and her daughters) and I will turn back the rejection of Samaria and her daughters. And I will turn back your rejection in their midst so that you should bear your pain and be disgraced for all that you did to make me angry.**
>
> **And your sister Sodom and her daughters shall be restored just as they were from the beginning. And Samaria and her daughters shall be restored just as they were from the beginning. And you and your daughters will be restored just as you were from the beginning.**[181]

In the passage above, God prophesies that: Because of his having clemency on the chosen ones' sins, he will have clemency on the disobedient 'non-chosen' ones. This is the very same concept that Paul wrote about in Romans chapter eleven. So we find that Paul's teaching comes from the Jewish scriptures.

But this information likely leaves the modern reader with more questions than answers. After all, if Christians are to have a special reward, then how can everyone be reconciled to God? On the surface, the two ideas appear mutually exclusive. However, these concepts

181 Ezekiel 16:46-55 translated from the Greek Septuagint; the version of the Jewish scriptures read and quoted by Paul. For a discussion on the different versions of the Jewish scriptures, see chapter 34, "Paul's Bible."

don't have to be mutually exclusive, *so long as they occur at different times.*

The Jewish culture believed in a future, *temporary* Messianic Age. The resurrected righteous will be raised immortal, living throughout the entire age right on into the next. However, the unrighteous will be raised with mortal bodies (just like their first ones), which will be punished in Gehenna, and then suffer the second death *for the forgiveness of their sins.*[182] They won't be re-resurrected with immortal bodies until the end of the Messianic Age, so that *only the righteous enjoy the life of the age to come.*

There were six Christian schools established during the first five hundred years of Christianity. They are listed below. I want you to circle which one(s) taught that the next age is an *eternal* age.

- The Christian school of Alexandria
- The Christian school of Antioch
- The Christian school of Cesarea
- The Christian school of Edessa
- The Christian school of Ephesus
- The Christian school of Rome

If you circled only the Christian school of Rome, you are correct. During the first five hundred years of Christianity, its beliefs represented the tiniest sliver of the faith. (Only later did it come to be the dominant theology through force—i.e. believe in the Latin doctrine based on misinterpreted Hebraisms, or die.)

The vast majority of Koine Greek-reading Christians understood the Bible taught that Jesus was coming back to usher in a finite Messianic Age (that will later be followed by the Eternal Age of God). They were more in touch with the Jewish Hebraisms than the

182 "This sin shall not be forgiven you until you die the second death."—Isaiah Targum 22:14. (Targums were the official religious teachings corresponding to each verse of scripture. This entry, therefore, was the official religious commentary on Isaiah 22:14.)

Latin school.

A full treatise on the doctrine of universal reconciliation is beyond the scope of this book. However, there is one particular teaching of Paul's that sheds tremendous light on both this teaching and Paul's message to the Predestined Proud. It shows how Paul concurred with the Jewish concept of ages. So let me introduce you to the Pauline version of the Stages of the Ages.

- The current age is the **Church Age**.
- Jesus will come back to usher in the **Messianic Age**.
- After which the **Eternal Age** of God will begin.

At the time Paul wrote Romans, he mentioned that he was revealing a "secret teaching." But, fortunately, three years later, he wrote a letter to the Corinthians in which he detailed how the once secret teaching will unfold. (Perhaps, the Corinthians had asked him to explain it, now that Paul had let the cat out of the bag three years prior, in his letter to the Romans.) Paul explains the timetable as follows:

> For just as in Adam all die, so also in Christ all shall be made alive, but each in their own order:
>
> > The Messianic King as the first fruit.
> >
> > After that those who are the Messianic King's at his coming.
> >
> > After that, at the conclusion, when he hands over the Kingdom to God the Father (at the time he has abolished all rule and all governance and all power).
>
> For he must reign until he has put all of his enemies under his feet. The last enemy that will be abolished is death.
>
> Now the prophecy says, "He gets all things subordinated to his authority under his feet." And while it says "all things are subordinated to his authority" it is clear that he himself is excepted; the one getting all things subordinated to himself. Once all things are subordinated to his authority, then the son will subordinate himself to the one who subordinated all

things to him, so that God may be all in all.[183]

There you have it: the timetable of universal reconciliation. Just as in Adam all humanity was made mortal, so also in Christ all humanity will be made immortal, *but each in its own order*. The body of the Messianic King was immortalized toward the beginning of the Church Age. Those who belong to Jesus will be immortalized at the beginning of the Messianic Age. Then, after Jesus gets the rest of humanity subordinated to his authority, they will be immortalized right before the Eternal Age of God—"at the conclusion, when Jesus hands over the Kingdom to God the Father." Then Jesus will subordinate himself to God's authority so that God may be all in *all*.

God will be all in all. God will be in everyone. That's Paul's description of the final state of the universe. However, prior to this happening, humanity will be divided into two groups during the Messianic Age: those rewarded with the life of the age[184] and those receiving the punishment of the age.[185]

Israel was prophesied to be the ones chosen to have the life of the Messianic Age. However, natural-born Israelites were blinded by God because he foreknew their rejection of Jesus (because of their obsession with the Jobs of the Law). Chosen Gentiles were grafted in their place, so they could have the life of the Messianic Age.

But some of these Gentiles were gloating over their election, putting down unbelieving Jews. Paul was displeased with their rotten attitude. So he informed these gloating Gentiles that this isn't the end of the story. After the Messianic Age is over, the cutoff Jews will be reconciled to God so that God may be all in all. God imprisoned everyone (the chosen and the cutoff) in disobedience so that he might have mercy on everyone (the chosen and the cutoff). This teaching was already foreshadowed in Ezekiel. Paul even outlined the timetable later in his letter to the Corinthians.

---

183 1 Corinthians 15:22-28

184 The Jewish idiom of life in *Olam Haba* (life in the age to come) became the Koine Greek Hebraism *aionios zoe.*

185 The Jewish idiom of punishment in *Olam Haba* (punishment in the age to come) became the Koine Greek Hebraism *aionios kolasis*

Most original Christians understood Paul's teaching perfectly (with the notable exception of some leaders in Rome). But, in the fifth century, Jerome (a Latin Church Father) finally succeeded in getting Christianity to replace Universal Reconciliation with the teaching of Eternal Damnation. The Christian faith was never the same since.

Why did Jerome do this? His lack of awareness of Hebraisms caused him to misunderstand the Bible's teachings on the punishment of the wicked:

- The Bible contains the Hebraism *punishment of the age,* which meant punishment in the age to come.[186] Jerome thought it meant *eternal punishment.*

- The Bible contains the Hebraism *Gehenna,* which meant temporary punishment in the fires of purgatory.[187, 188] Jerome thought it referred to a place of eternal damnation.

- The Bible contains the Hebraism *second death,* which referred to the death of the resurrected body (not soul) **for the forgiveness of sins.**[189] Jerome thought the phrase symbolized the eternal inability to ever have the sins forgiven.

So Jerome's lack of Hebraisms caused him to make mistakes. He permanently altered the course of Christianity through a combination of focused will and lack of knowledge. Later, the Protestant Reformers

186 The early Jewish religious literature shows that the Jews expected a coming temporary Messianic Age. "The world is to exist six thousand years. In the first two thousand there was desolation; two thousand years the Torah flourished; and the next two thousand years is the Messianic era"—Sanhedrin 97a. In early Jewish thought, resurrected humanity will either have *life in the Messianic Era* (Hebraism *aionios zoe*) or *punishment in the Messianic Era* (Hebraism *aionios kolasis*). Jerome's lack of knowledge regarding Hebraisms caused him to mistakenly think these terms referred to 'eternal life' and 'eternal punishment.' Orthodox Christianity has been following Jerome's error ever since.

187 "The duration of the punishment of the wicked in Gehenna is twelve months." - Shabbat 33b (an ancient Jewish writing)

188 "The judgment on the generation of the Flood was for twelve months, on Job for twelve months, on the Egyptians for twelve months, on Gog and Magog in the Hereafter for twelve months, and on the wicked in Gehenna for twelve months." - Mishna Eduyot 2:10; Genesis Rabbah 28:8 (ancient Jewish writings)

189 "This sin shall not be forgiven you until you die the second death."—Isaiah Targum 22:14. (Targums were the official religious teachings corresponding to each verse of scripture. This entry, therefore, was the official religious commentary on Isaiah 22:14.)

came along and embraced Jerome's mistaken ideas. Due to their lack of knowledge regarding even the prior existence of Koine Greek, they added many mistakes of their own. Then they permanently altered the course of the Christian faith through their own combination of focused will and lack of knowledge. And here we are today.

Appendix C
Other Puzzles Solved

The Jerome Conspiracy parable pieces together the unwritten history on how the doctrine of eternal punishment became part of the Christian Bible and faith.

The Hidden Bible parable pieces together the exact identity of 666.

The Jesus Secret pieces together information revealed in the Koine papyri to recover Jesus' one teaching that unites the entire New Testament together. *The Jesus Secret* was the precursor to *Breaking the Romans Code*, and is an exploration of the same topic from the Koine papyri perspective. Through *The Jesus Secret* and *Breaking the Romans Code* combined, readers are exposed to the full range of archaeological discoveries which prove that Jesus' original teaching truly had been buried for almost two thousand years … until now.

Bibliography

Bromiley, Geoffrey W. *The International Standard Bible Encyclopedia*. Grand Rapids, MI: Eerdmans, 1995. Print.

Bucher, Dr. Richard P. "Reformation Day." *St. Paul's Lutheran Church of Kingsville, MD (LCMS)*. Web. 20 Mar. 2011. <http://www.stpaulskingsville.org/reformation.htm>. See article entitled "Martin Luther's Tower Experience."

Calvin, John, and William Pringle. *Commentary on a Harmony of the Evangelists, Matthew, Mark, and Luke: Volume First ; Commentary on a Harmony of the Evangelists, Matthew, Mark, and Luke : Volume Second*. Grand Rapids, MI: Baker, 2003. Print.

Cribiore, Raffaella. *Gymnastics of the Mind: Greek Education in Hellenistic and Roman Egypt*. Princeton, NJ: Princeton UP, 2001. Print.

Cross, F. L., and Elizabeth A. Livingstone. *The Oxford Dictionary of the Christian Church*. Oxford: Oxford UP, 2005. Print.

Danker, Frederick W., Walter Bauer, and William Arndt. *A Greek-English Lexicon of the New Testament and Other Early Christian Literature*. Chicago: University of Chicago, 2000. Print.

Daube, David. *The New Testament and Rabbinic Judaism*. New York: Arno, 1973. Print.

Diamant, Anita, and Howard Cooper. *Living a Jewish Life: Jewish Traditions, Customs, and Values for Today's Families*. New York, NY: HarperCollins, 2007. Print.

Eisenberg, Joyce, and Ellen Scolnic. *Dictionary of Jewish Words*. Philadelphia: Jewish Publication Society, 2006. Print.

Eisenberg, Ronald L. *What the Rabbis Said: 250 Topics from the Talmud*. Santa Barbara, CA: Praeger, 2010. Print.

Freedman, David Noel, Allen C. Myers, and Astrid B. Beck. *Eerdmans Dictionary of the Bible*. Grand Rapids, MI: W.B. Eerdmans, 2000. Print.

Gordis, Robert. *The Dynamics of Judaism: a Study in Jewish Law.* Bloomington: Indiana UP, 1990. Print.

Green, Joel B., Scot McKnight, and I. Howard. Marshall. *Dictionary of Jesus and the Gospels.* Leicester: InterVarsity, 1992. Print.

Horsley, G. H. R. *New Documents Illustrating Early Christianity: Linguistic Essays.* Macquarie University, N.S.W.: Ancient History Documentary Research Centre, Macquarie University, 1989. Print.

Keener, Craig S. *A Commentary on the Gospel of Matthew.* Grand Rapids, MI: W.B. Eerdmans Pub., 1999. Print.

Lachs, Samuel Tobias. *A Rabbinic Commentary on the New Testament: the Gospels of Matthew, Mark, and Luke.* Hoboken, NJ: KTAV Pub. House, 1987. Print.

Milavec, Aaron. *The Didache: Text, Translation, Analysis, and Commentary.* Collegeville, MN: Liturgical, 2004. Print.

Pasachoff, Naomi E., Jody Wheeler, Marlies Najaka, Lesley Silverstone, Lois Miller. Cohn, Cynthia F. Reich, and Michael Zeldin. *Basic Judaism for Young People.* West Orange, NJ: Behrman House, 1986. Print.

Schneier, Bruce. *Applied Cryptography: Protocols, Algorithms, and Source Code in C.* New York: Wiley, 1996. Print.

Smith, Sir William, and Henry Wace. *A Dictionary of Christian Biography: Literature, Sects and Doctrines...* London: John Murray., 1877. Print.

Vermes, Geza. *The Complete Dead Sea Scrolls in English.* London: Penguin, 2004. Print.

Young, Brad H. *Meet the Rabbis Rabbinic Thought and the Teachings of Jesus.* Grand Rapids, MI: Baker Academic, 2007. Print.

Yust, Karen-Marie. *Nurturing Child and Adolescent Spirituality: Perspectives from the World's Religious Traditions.* Lanham, MD: Rowman & Littlefield, 2006. Print.

LaVergne, TN USA
28 March 2011
221864LV00002B/1/P